ARK

BALTI

•Rostock

Lübeck•   •Wismar

amburg

nke

R. Elbe

edel
hlinteln
hem

E A S T

R. Oder

P O L A N D

R. Aller
H

BERLIN

Hannover

G E R M A N Y

Braunschweig

Goslar•
lzminden

•Wittenberg

assel

•Hammelburg

affenburg

•Würzburg

E   R   I   C   A,   N

•Nuremberg

ilbronn
•Crailsheim

Neckargemund

ttgart   Z   O   N   E

B A V A R I A

ngen

•Regensberg

PRAGUE

C Z E C H O S L O V A K I A

•Pilsen

VIENNA

A U S T R I A

Munich

Miles

0   50   100

BLOODY BREMEN

BLOODY BREMEN
Ike's Last Stand

'It is a delusion to imagine that a plan of campaign can be
laid down far ahead and fulfilled with exactitude. The
first collision with the enemy creates a new situation in
accordance with the result. Some things intended will
have become impracticable. Others which originally
seemed impossible become feasible.'

Helmuth von Moltke

by

CHARLES WHITING

LEO COOPER
LONDON

First published in Great Britain in 1998 by
LEO COOPER
an imprint of
Pen & Sword Books Ltd
47 Church Street
Barnsley
South Yorkshire
S70 2AS

ISBN 0 85052 595 0

A catalogue record for this book is
available from the British Library

Typeset in 11/13pt Candida
by Phoenix Typesetting, Ilkley, West Yorkshire

Printed and bound in Great Britain by
Mackays of Chatham PLC, Chatham, Kent

FOR
LEO COOPER
AND TOM HARTMAN

CONTENTS

ACKNOWLEDGEMENTS

My thanks are due to the *Weser Kurier*, Bremen, New York Public Library System and, in particular, to Tom Dickinson, Carl Sillitoe, Fred Pettinger of the 52nd Reconnaissance Regiment, OCA, to Hy Schorr and all the others, sadly long dead, from my old Corps Commander, General Horrocks, through to Chas Bedford of the 53rd Division, Tom Jones of the 6th Airborne and the not-so-lamented 'last Führer', Grand Admiral Karl Doenitz.

Charles Whiting

'There is only one thing worse than fighting with allies – and that is fighting without them.'

Winston Churchill, March, 1945

ECLIPSE

On the evening of Monday, 5 March, 1945, 55-year-old Colonel-
General Jodl returned to his Berlin flat after a hard day with the
Führer discussing the situation on the Rhine, where it was clear
that the Western Allies would soon begin their long-planned
crossing of Germany's last natural bulwark. There had been the
usual American raid on Berlin and it had taken him ages to get
back from the High Command in the Bendlerstrasse. Jodl,
Hitler's Chief-of-Operations, was very tired, but there was no
escaping what he had to do that cold March night.

A drink, a shave, a fresh shirt, and he was off again in his staff
car to the apartment of his future wife, Louise von Bender.
Louise, now in her late thirties, had served him loyally as his
personal secretary throughout the war, and latterly as his
mistress. Indeed, such was his confidence in her that she knew
more state secrets than many a general. Since his wife, the
former Countess von Bullion, had died as the result of an operation on her spine, he had come to rely upon the sympathetic
Louise even more.

Louise admitted him to her cold, cheerless flat – coal was
running out yet again – and after some talk about their forthcoming marriage, he opened his briefcase and took out a
red-covered dossier with the legend printed across it in black
'Geheime Reichssache'.* It ran to seventy pages, with two maps
attached. Silently he handed it to Louise.

There are various explanations as to how this vital Allied

---

* Roughly 'Top Secret'.

document fell into German hands; but, as far as Jodl was concerned, it had been taken from a shot-up British armoured vehicle of the British XXX Corps during the final stages of the Battle of the Bulge late in January, 1945. Then he said to Louise, 'That's what the Allies intend to do with Germany.'

She looked down at the document. Hitler himself had spent a whole evening the previous month poring over it before deciding that it should be classified 'State Top Secret', to be studied *only* by his leading military advisers and their staffs. He felt that the details of the Allied intentions which the document revealed were too much even for the toughest of his field commanders.

Louise had seen plenty of maps in her time and this one didn't look much different from the others – save for two things: the map of Germany had lines drawn across it and the lettering was in English.

Her heart sank as she realized that she was holding in her hand the Allied blueprint for the enemy occupation of Germany once the Third Reich had been defeated. It sank even further when Jodl translated the word stamped across the folder; OPERATION ECLIPSE. That summarized everything. If the enemy won the war, this was to be Germany's future.

Jodl took the folder from his fiancée's hands and said, 'That's what they intend. Look at the new frontiers.'

She studied the black boundary lines drawn across the map. The north and north-east, from Cologne on the Rhine to Hamburg and Bremen on the Elbe and Weser, bore the initials 'U.K.'. The south, including Hesse and Bavaria, from the River Main at Frankfurt to the border with Italy and Austria were stamped 'U.S.A.', and, between the two, roughly the whole of Central Germany, was stamped 'U.S.S.R.'. This was to be the future division of Germany between the 'Big Three'. Louise looked at her future husband, aghast. 'It's like a nightmare,' she whispered. Then she asked him where the file had come from. His reply was typically evasive. He said the documents were definitely genuine, but he wouldn't reveal how they had been obtained, except to say that 'We got them from a British Headquarters', an answer which seems to heighten the mystery.

2

What would a combat headquarters be doing carrying top secret documents into battle?

In due course Jodl returned to the Bendlerstrasse. Hitler, who often did not get up until midday, liked to have a later briefing before he got down to his long and boring nocturnal monologues or the girlie films from Hollywood which Goebbels provided, although films of that kind were forbidden in Nazi Germany. Jodl always liked to be ready in case Hitler asked any awkward questions, which he frequently did.

Left by herself, Louise brooded on what she had just seen. Only after an hour did she suddenly realize that if Germany were beaten, her relations who lived in the Hartz Mountains east of Goslar, would be part of the future Russian Zone of Occupation. She was faced with an agonizing decision. Should she betray Alfred's confidence and warn her relatives to flee while there was still time? The Red Army was already fighting on the River Oder, which separated Germany from what had once been Poland. She decided for the family. She couldn't allow her sister-in-law and four small children to fall into the hands of the Russians. She rang her and remarked, as casually as she could, 'You know the east wind is very strong these days. I really think you and the children should move west beyond the river.' Her sister-in-law didn't understand one word of the veiled warning, but Louise worried for days, wondering when that fateful knock on the door would come, indicating that the Gestapo had been listening to the conversation. But they never came and she lived to support her husband through the long, bitter trial at Nuremberg until Master-Sergeant Wood, the official US Army hangman, came late one night to place the noose round Jodl's neck.

Operation 'Eclipse' was a general plan to take over Germany in the event of a sudden surrender or collapse. It had started before D-Day under the codename 'Talisman'. In November, 1944, it had been drawn up by Roosevelt and, three months later, at Yalta, had been ratified by the 'Big Three' – Roosevelt, Churchill and Stalin.

Although 'Eclipse' revealed some of the Allies' military plans in case of a sudden breakdown of the Third Reich, it dealt primarily with more mundane matters such as armistice and the problem of displaced prisoners of war. However, the two maps attached to the text, plus a covering letter signed by Montgomery's Chief-of-Staff, General de Guingand, did give a great deal of military-political information. Politically, it was clear that the way in which Dr Goebbels, the Minister of Propaganda, was predicting an imminent breakdown of the Western Alliance was wrong. It might well be that Churchill was highly suspicious of Russian motives in Western Europe, alarmed by communist agitation in France, Belgium and Italy, and, in the case of Greece, open warfare between the communist underground and British troops in Athens. But the document made it clear that there was complete unity between the Big Three on the German question.

The first paragraph of De Guingand's letter stated: 'In order to carry out the surrender terms imposed on Germany, the governments of the United States, the United Kingdom . . . and the Soviet Union have agreed that Germany is to be occupied by the Armed Forces of the three powers'. Disagree they might about spheres of influence, but not about the fate of Germany. 'The only possible answer to the trumpets of total war,' the document maintained, 'is total defeat and total occupation!'

The maps supported this point of view, though they revealed little of Allied military intentions. Still, they *did* indicate that the Western Allies would stick to their agreed-upon zones of occupation. Indeed, just after the Allies crossed the Rhine Jodl played a hunch based on his study of the covering letter and the maps. After lunch one day he remarked to Louise, now his wife, that, as she had seen, the line of demarcation between the Western Allies and the Red Army ran from north to south along the line of the River Elbe from below Lübeck to Wittenberg. From there it curled south-west towards Eisenach before swinging due east to the German–Czech border.

Louise nodded, and then her husband played his hunch. He asked, rhetorically, if the demarcation line between the future Russian and Anglo-American zones of Occupation also marked the limits of the British and American drive eastwards. Of course she didn't know the answer – not that Jodl had expected her to. But he himself was quite certain that this line would mark the furthest Anglo-American penetration into Central Germany.

4

With certain exceptions, due to the natural chaos of battle, especially the fluid kind of warfare sought by armoured units, the Allies would halt on that line, that is if the map had *really* been captured from an advanced British headquarters during the last stages of the Battle of the Bulge.

Jodl told his wife that he didn't think the Americans and the British were heading for Berlin at all. Instead, he believed, they were leaving the capture of what Eisenhower had always called the 'glittering prize' to the Russians. In short, unless the 'Eclipse' maps had been changed since they had fallen into German hands, it looked as if Eisenhower's armies would come to a halt on that boundary line. Without the prize of Berlin, which was going to be left to the Russians, what was there for the Anglo-Americans to fight for?

At this time, March, 1945, Eisenhower, the Allied Supreme Commander, was floundering. President Roosevelt, his Commander-in-Chief, four thousand miles away in Washington, was a dying man. He who should have been making the key political decisions on Europe's future was simply drifting along, being kept artificially alive by his doctors. The only other man capable of taking decisions General George Marshall, the head of the Army in Washington, had little interest in the politics of post-war Europe. He was now more concerned, since Germany appeared to be virtually defeated, with the future conduct of the war against Japan. He was already bombarding Eisenhower with requests for key personnel to be sent to the Pacific and had ensured that Eisenhower set up an agency in Europe to earmark veteran US infantry outfits for that theatre.

In essence the conduct of the rest of the war in Europe was left in the hands of the Supreme Commander. But, like his master in Washington, Ike had little interest in the political affairs of a post-war Europe. His main concern was to win the war and at the same time to stop the open squabbling between his generals that had been threatening ever since the Battle of the Bulge the previous January when he had been forced to give the command of more US divisions to Montgomery than were commanded by Bradley, his US Army Group chief. That month had seen victory in the Ardennes, but had also marked a turning point in Anglo-American relations. Since then both Bradley and his flamboyant subordinate, Patton, had told Eisenhower that they would rather resign than ever serve under Montgomery again. Now, in March, with the crossing of the Rhine looming ever larger, they had persistently urged Eisenhower that it was a matter of 'American prestige' that the US Army should be given the kudos of final victory on the other side of the river. Montgomery was to be cut out, or, at the most, given an insignificant rôle.

Since the war the literature of that conflict has generally portrayed Ike as a somewhat naive, inexperienced battlefield commander, who originated in the sticks, but had the gift of being able to make such disparate allies as Britain and France work successfully together with the American Army. In fact, Eisenhower was not as naive as he is made out. Even before he left Abilene for the big world, he had canvassed important local citizens to get him the all-important appointment to West Point. In Washington, in the late '20s and early '30s, his brothers lobbied for him as an ideal candidate for a staff post. In later years his critics pointed out scornfully that the Supreme Commander had never commanded so much as a platoon in action throughout his career. But Eisenhower had done something more important. He had been on the staff, where he had got to know the people who would be vitally important for his career if and when a war came.

Now he had to make a decision about the conduct of the war which would appease his rebellious US generals and ensure that his prestige back home would be high enough to make him appear the obvious candidate to succeed General Marshall.* To do this it would be necessary to abandon the long-planned attack on Berlin. Any drive across Northern Germany would, by the nature of things at the front, come under the command of Montgomery. Besides, 'Eclipse' made it clear that the Big Three had agreed that the capture of Berlin would be left to the Red Army. What rôle then could the US Army assume, especially as 'Eclipse' also envisaged the capture of most of Central Germany being carried out by the Russians?

---

* Though by this time Patton had already observed to his staff that Ike was 'bucking for President'.

So the concept of the 'National Redoubt' was born, as if of necessity. It was supposed that large numbers of fanatical Nazis were being gathered in a defensive position in the Bavarian-Austrian Alps, where they might well hold out for years. At the time Bradley maintained that the US Army might still be fighting in the mountains in 1946!

On 20 March, in a message to the US War Department, Eisenhower observed, 'We could launch a movement to the south-east to prevent Nazi occupation of Nazi citadel.' This 'citadel' proved illusory, and Bradley, writing, probably tongue in cheek, after the war, lamented, 'Not until after the campaign ended were we to learn that this Redoubt existed largely in the imagination of a few fanatic Nazis.* It grew into so exaggerated a scheme that I am astonished we could have believed it as innocently as we did. But while it persisted, this legend of the Redoubt was too ominous a threat to be ignored and in consequence it shaped our tactical thinking during the closing weeks of the war.'

In essence, under the 'Eclipse' plan Eisenhower need not have done anything. All the soul-searching about whether he should or should not have gone on to Berlin, which has featured so prominently in the histories of the war in Europe over the last fifty years, was pointless. Left to his own devices, Eisenhower could have halted his troops on the 'Eclipse' line and waited for the Russians to carry out their part in the agreed plan.

But he had not reckoned with his generals. As General Gavin, commander of the US 82nd Airborne Division, wrote, 'The American generals had the strength and they intended to use it to win the war in the manner they considered to be in the US interest.'

One of those generals put it more succinctly. In 1945, immediately after the events of that spring, General Patton wrote, 'We all felt it was essential that the First and Third Armies should get themselves so involved that Montgomery's plan to use most of the divisions on the Western front, British and American, under his command . . . could not come off.'

---

* Bradley might have added, 'In the imagination of most American generals too'.

Thus it was that in the last week of March, 1945, some two weeks before the death of President Roosevelt, who might have exerted some restraining influence if he had lived, Eisenhower launched his 1st, 3rd and 7th Armies on a massive wild-goose chase across central and southern Germany to attack a fortress which didn't exist.

Over the next month some two million American soldiers fought from one German city to another. Each of them, from Mannheim to Munich, had been declared a *Festung* (fortress) by Hitler and each of them took up to a week to capture. Naturally each of them claimed scores, sometimes hundreds, of young American lives. And to what purpose? The 'Redoubt', as we have seen, was a myth. The capture of these cities, virtually all of which could have been bypassed, served no political purpose whatsoever and had absolutely no influence on events in postwar Europe.

So what was the point? The capture of each new 'fortress' enhanced the reputation and prestige of the US Army and gave the generals concerned the headlines they craved back in the States. In the postwar US Army battles won would mean promotion, and for a regular soldier nothing is more important than that.

But what of Montgomery's rôle in all this? To his astonishment the man who had recently commanded twenty US divisions in the Battle of the Bulge and helped Eisenhower by pulling the chestnuts out of the fire for him was relegated to the rôle of flank guard. It was to be the task of his British 21st Army Group to protect Bradley's rear and flank from any counter-attack through Holland, as the US 12th Army Group advanced towards the 'Redoubt'. Montgomery was being given a trip to the seaside!

Indeed, when he started his progress north with a relatively weak 2nd British Army, Montgomery seemed to have only one real objective – the capture of the city of Bremen and the port of Bremerhaven. The US Army would need a main supply port for the American Army of Occupation in Germany, and, based on the French record of obstruction in the last few weeks, Eisenhower felt that he could not depend on them to keep, Marseilles and Cherbourg, at the time the two major supply ports, open. Hence Montgomery was urged to capture the Bremen-Bremerhaven complex for postwar American use. So it came about that the British were given the only objective of some value in a campaign that would involve one British, one Canadian and four US armies. Bremen was, it seemed, the only 'fortress' that had any military-political significance whatsoever.

What happened next seemed to bear out the American Top Brass. Montgomery would fight a series of bitter actions. The casualties would be high. In fact there were 21,646 British and Canadian casualties between the crossings of the Rhine and the Elbe out of a total of 191,219 for the campaign as a whole, a campaign neglected by British military historians and regarded by the Americans as something of a walkover.

Why was this campaign, 'Monty's last battle', and perhaps the last battle of any importance that the British Army will ever fight, regarded as something of an irrelevance, especially by the Americans? Was it just a sop to British national prestige as so many US commentators have regarded it?

Stephen E. Ambrose, the American historian, has written in his *Supreme Command*, a study of Eisenhower, that 'by stressing Lübeck [to Montgomery] he gave Twenty-First Army Group a significant rôle to play, which hopefully would mollify the British'. Bradley, who apparently ended the war hating Montgomery, wrote maliciously that 'Monty's last campaign from the Rhine to Lübeck was, on the whole, one of the most cautious and uninspired of the war. It began with the flamboyant overkill of the Rhine in a typical Monty set-piece battle and petered out to his usual desultory pursuit and reluctance to go for the jugular, to make the kill, to take risks. Had we not primed Ridgway* in advance and then rushed him to help Monty, the Russians would have surely reached the Danish border first and perhaps gone on to Copenhagen with possible damaging consequences in the post-war world.'

This is rich coming from a general who at the time showed not one bit of interest for the politics of postwar Europe and who

* General Matthew B. Ridgway, commander of the Allied XVIII Airborne Corps.

frittered away the massive resources of the US Army on a wild-goose chase for the mythical redoubt.

One popular American historian, John Toland, gently mocked the whole campaign in the north in his *The Last Hundred Days*: 'For the past few weeks Blumentritt [Monty's opponent in the North] had been waging a gentleman's battle with the British . . . with as little bloodshed as possible. Since mid-April an informal liaison officer from Second British Army came to Blumentritt unofficially and said that since the Russians were closing in on Lübeck, His Majesty's Forces wondered if the Germans would allow them to take the Baltic port ahead of the Russians.'

Toland should have told that to the 1st Monmouths or the 1/5th Welch, battalions originally some 800 strong cut down by the end of the campaign to about 200 men apiece, most of them green reinforcements. Not exactly the result of a gentlemanly campaign between His Majesty's Forces and the kindly Germans.

In fact, Montgomery's forgotten campaign in the north was really fought to prevent the Russians making too many gains. It was conducted against a background of such national and personal pride and Anglo-American rivalry that one wonders who the enemy was – the Germans, the Russians or, in effect, the Americans.

Nor did Montgomery help. After the war Eisenhower remarked that Monty irritated him like 'a burr under a saddle' and that for six whole weeks he had refused to speak to him. On the British side, Sir James Grigg, the Minister of War and a personal friend of Montgomery, warned the latter just before the war ended to stop his personal attacks on the Americans. On a 'one-time' cipher pad Grigg wrote to him: 'I beseech you in the bowels of Christ to watch your step, or at any rate your loud-speaker, as long as SHAEF [Eisenhower's Allied HQ] exists. I have quite enough quarrels to cope with.'

In the end Montgomery's April drive northwards and the little-known campaign he fought resulted in a great victory for the British – and their American allies. The capture of Bremen led to the surrender of its sister Hansa port of Hamburg, which in its turn resulted in the capitulation of all German forces in

Northern Germany and finally in Germany as a whole. The Anglo-Americans had forced Germany to surrender, not the Red Army, as had been expected. And the greatest surprise of all was that Montgomery, relegated, so it seemed, to an obscure flank in the north, had caused it all to happen.

BOOK ONE

AACHEN TO NUREMBERG

They grant us sudden days,
Snatched from the business of war.
We are too close to appraise
What manner of men they are.

Rudyard Kipling.

1

SEPTEMBER – OCTOBER, 1944

I

IF WE HAVE TO DIE,
YOU CAN DIE TOO

Peace, it seemed, had descended upon the ruined city at last. The magnificent oaks, which had once graced Aachen's avenues, were gashed and broken. Great chunks of 18th century stonework lay on all sides. After five weeks of fighting, the streets were littered with the débris of battle, the twisted wrecks of armoured vehicles, burned-out trucks and jeeps, abandoned equipment and bundles of rags which had once been young men.

Now the only sound was the distant rumble of artillery on the outskirts of the city and the occasional crump of high explosive as the Germans destroyed key installations. But the sudden lull after weeks of bitter fighting was misleading. For both sides were now preparing for the final round. The besieged city had only fifty-seven hours to live.

The triumphant Americans had first crossed the German border at six o'clock on the evening of Monday, 11 September, 1944. The Battle for Aachen had started. In the following weeks veteran US divisions such as the 1st and 30th Infantry and the 3rd Armoured Division had been brought to a virtual standstill. For this was a prestige objective for both the German and American armies. It was the first major German city that the US Army had attacked in the Second World War. But now the end was nigh.

SS Major Rink of the elite 1st SS Panzer Division used the lull to withdraw from Aachen's main battle headquarters. Colonel Wilck, the Commandant, had already left and Rink decided that

17

he wasn't going to sacrifice his young troopers in defence of an empty HQ. He assembled the fifty ragged survivors of *Kampfgrüppe Rink*, who had been smuggled into the besieged city two weeks before and told them they would be leaving by the main entrance; the Americans wouldn't expect that. Under cover of a low wall, they would crawl to the next intersection. Here they would rush the street in small groups. He knew, of course, that the crossroads was under permanent enemy fire, but he hoped that the sudden German breakout would take the Americans by surprise. With luck the first escapers would make it. As for those who came later – well, he didn't want to think about that.

But there were no objections from Rink's young soldiers who would have followed him to hell and back. They knew he had been through this sort of thing often enough in the past. If anyone could get them through safely, it would be Rink.

It was growing dark when they left the HQ and the Americans didn't even hear them go. They crawled along the side of the wall to the crossroads without a shot being fired at them. Rink had guessed right. Now they gathered together for the last stage of the breakout. As Rink had predicted, the crossroads was under permanent fire. Further up the street, where it bent slightly, the Americans had set up several half-inch machine guns which hammered away constantly. Rink drew a deep breath and grasped his pistol firmly in a hand damp with sweat. 'All right,' he ordered above the high-pitched snarl of the machine guns,' You, you and you, you're coming with me in the first group. If we get across the rest of you will follow at irregular intervals. Here we go!'

Stooped low, the four SS men broke cover. The machine gunners reacted a fraction of a second too late. Before they could open up, the men had flung themselves into the brick rubble of the other side of the road. They had made it.

Rink waved his hand urgently at the next group waiting to cross. Now it was tricky, but there was no going back. They took a deep breath and pelted across. Again they made it. Another group followed, and another.

Now it was the turn of Peter Schaaf, a handsome young trooper from Aachen itself who would later record the escape of

Battle Group Rink for posterity. He looked at his comrades' faces and knew they were thinking exactly the same as he was. This time the American machine-gunners would certainly be ready for them.

Schaaf sprang forward and ran as he had never run before. To his right the NCO in charge of the group groaned and flung up his hands. Nobody stopped to help him. The next moment Schaaf slammed into the bullet-pocked wall on the other side of the street. He had done it!

Half an hour later the fifty survivors of SS Battle Group Rink were setting up their new headquarters in the cellars of Number 17 Weyerstrasse while Schaaf and his mates toiled away to break into the cellar of the next house, 'mouse-holing' they called it. Little did he realize that, years later, he would be delivering heating oil to that very house!

That same afternoon another Aachener, older, fatter and quite happy with what was happening to him, was forced out of a similar cellar at bayonet point. Six weary GIs of the US 1st Division brought the 52-year-old civilian up to street level where he told them, 'I am the Bishop of Aachen.' The one GI equipped with a walkie-talkie contacted his CO and asked what they should do with him. Colonel Corley, the Battalion Commander, answered promptly, 'Treat him like a general.'

Bishop Johannes van der Welden knew they would look after him well because of his influence over Aachen's catholic population. But for the time being the news of the Bishop's 'rescue' or 'capture', whichever way you looked at it, was kept secret on orders of the US 1st Army. The Allied correspondents who were now flooding into the ruined city to report its imminent capture were forced to rely on trivia, though even that seemed at the time to be indicative of the way the war in Europe was going, now that the Germans had been driven back across their own frontier.

The reporter of the London *Daily Express* noted that a 'soldier with a wooden arm and a captain, blind in one eye, and unable to see well in the other' were captured that day. Reuters' correspondent gave the details of his interview with a 25-year-old German deserter, who told him, 'Four years of war are enough.

19

We have had no water in Aachen for four days. The electricity is smashed. We have been collecting rainwater or water from a pool. There is still plenty of food in many houses. Many of the [surrender] leaflets fired into the town yesterday drifted away, but the word went around. The officers stopped us talking to the civilians and orders were given to fire on any civilian trying to leave the city. One NCO leaving with me was fired on by the SS. But we got away with one man wounded.' The man added that young fanatics had fired on those of their comrades who wanted to give up because, 'if we have to die, you can die too'.

If the newspaper correspondents were to be believed, the final breakdown had arrived, and Hitler also seemed to think so. In his radio message to the German people three days before, he had declared, 'After five years of struggle, the enemy, helped by the defection of our European allies, has at some points come near to Germany's frontiers and at others reached it. As in 1939, now we stand alone to meet the blows of our enemy. At that time we succeeded by the first large-scale mobilization of our people . . . We know the resolution of our Jewish international enemies to destroy us totally. We are meeting them with the total mobilization of all Germany . . . I call upon all German men able to carry a weapon to make themselves ready to fight!'

The German Home Guard, *der Volkssturm*, had been born. Every German male between the ages of 16 and 60 not already in the Armed Forces had to report for duty. It was the last levée. Optimists in the Allied camp were now predicting that Germany would be out of the war by Christmas.

General Clarence Huebner, the balding commander of the 1st US Infantry Division, known as The Big Red One, certainly hoped so. He had served in every rank in the 1st Division from enlisted man to commanding general and was now to launch the last attack on the besieged city. It was one that he was determined would succeed.

The 1st Infantry had fired the first shot of any American unit on a European battlefield exactly twenty-seven years before. It had also fired the first American shot in Africa in 1943. Now Huebner wanted it to have the honour of being the first to capture a major German city. They had suffered hundreds of casualties in street fighting in Aachen and Huebner felt they had

20

earned the right to bring it all to an end. So he ordered his two infantry commanders, Colonel Corley and Daniel, to prepare for the final assault on the morrow.

A mile away the Fortress Commander, Colonel Wilck, deep in his four-storey bunker in Aachen's ruined Rutscher-Forterstrasse, prepared what would be his last order of the day to the remaining 1,200 soldiers under his command. It read: 'The Defenders of Aachen will now prepare for the last battle. Forced back into the smallest possible space, we shall fight to the last man, the last grenade and the last bullet. In the face of the contemptible, despicable treason committed by certain individuals, I expect each and every one of the defenders of this venerable imperial city of Aachen to do his duty to the very end in fulfilment of our oath to the flag*. I expect courage and determination. Long live the Führer and our beloved Fatherland!'

---

* In the German Army the soldier swears an oath of loyalty on the flag, spread out in front of him, to his country and the Commander-in-Chief.

II

THERE ARE NO GODDAM
NAZIS HERE

Dawn over the shattered city came slowly, as if some God on high was reluctant to throw light on the devilish work of man below. The forecast was for a bright crisp autumn day, but the soldiers of the Big Red One were more concerned with the next few hours, which would decide whether they were to live or die.

The men who would lead the attack were dirty, unshaven and in no mood for conversation, save for a few grunts, quite unlike the dashing, wise-cracking heroes of Hollywood war movies. Crouched in their hiding places in the rubble of the shattered houses, they waited for the bloody business of killing and being killed to begin again.

During the night Colonel Wilck had made his last dispositions. Some of his officers had pleaded with him to surrender, but he had refused. He had a wife on the other side of the Rhine, held hostage by the Führer. If he wasn't seen to fight to the bitter end, she might well find herself behind bars. During the night he had been told he had been awarded Nazi Germany's highest honour, the Knight's Cross of the Iron Cross, and that fifteen Iron Crosses, First Class, and 147 Iron Crosses, Second Class, had been smuggled into his bunkers. A cynic might have laughed at the number of decorations: there were more of them than defenders of the bunker. But for Wilck the situation was too serious for laughter. He put on a clean uniform, complete with decorations, and told his orderly to pack a small suitcase with the things he would need when he was taken prisoner.

The first rumble of the American artillery had begun, accompanied by the thud of smaller mortar pieces. The bombs started to explode in the ruins as the enemy machine guns began to sweep them with bursts of tracer.

Over on the other side grumpy NCOs were clambering from position to position, whispering as if the Germans might overhear them: 'Okay guys. Five minutes to go, five minutes to go.' Then came the old, old cry they had heard so many times before: 'All right, you guys, *let's move it!*'

At his Advance Command Post in an Aachen suburb General Clarence Huebner was already awake and alert. He knew that the enemy was now compressed into a very small area of Aachen, perhaps only a mile square. From there they had only one axis of movement left open to them, the main road leading to Holland, the Roermonderstrasse. Huebner reckoned that the German command structure would break down once his men attacked. Then, he felt, the remaining pockets of German resistance, cut off from their officers, would surrender.

Two frightened German women, hiding in the ruins, were the first to spot the Americans advancing cautiously down the street. Then the one man in their hideout put up a white flag. Four weeks earlier he had narrowly escaped being shot by his own troops for doing the same thing, but the Americans relaxed when they saw it. This was going to be a walkover after all. A German-American searched the ruins for any German troops, and, when satisfied that there were none, told the man to copy out words he had just written down on to a large poster and put it over the twisted frame of the door. Half an hour later, as fresh troops passed into the attack, they laughed when they saw the sign which read THERE ARE NO GODDAM NAZIS HERE.

The GIs captured Wilck's former headquarters and pushed on to another strongpoint, this one still held by German paratroops. They knew the fanatical tenacity of the German *Fallschirmjäger* of old. 'No fooling with them,' Lieutenant William Batchford, leading the American point, shouted out. Then a huge 155mm cannon was called up and started to pound the paras' position at point blank range. Mortar, bricks and twisted steel girders flew everywhere. Surely no one could live through that barrage. But Batchford was taking no chances. He didn't want to take unnecessary casualties at this stage of the battle. While the gun pounded away, he led his men into the enemy stronghold, once a smart hotel.

The surprised paras ran upstairs, hand-to-hand fighting breaking out with those not quick enough to escape. Hand grenades whizzed back and forth. Slowly the Germans were pushed back, leaving their dead sprawled behind them, but still they refused to surrender.

Batchford, knowing that he was holding up the whole advance and with General Huebner breathing down his neck, called for machine guns. They went into action at once and poured a vicious stream of fire into the basement where the surviving paras were holding out. By now they'd had enough. With hands clasped behind their backs, the young fanatics came up, leaving twenty-five of their comrades lying dead below.

Batchford ran up the stairs of the once plush hotel. The men followed, stamping over broken glass and kicking aside the bullet-riddled chairs. A GI pushed a dead German gunner from the seat of his quadruple flak cannon used in a ground rôle, which the paras had taken to pieces and re-assembled on the upper floor. The GI swung it round and started to pour a stream of tracer at the German positions on the other side of the hotel grounds. The battle went on.

Meanwhile the senior officers of the Big Red One poked through the ruins in the hope that they might find the body of the city's Battle Commandant. But they were out of luck. Colonel Wilck had vanished and, without him, the Americans knew they couldn't get Aachen to surrender.

In his new HQ Colonel Wilck had just interviewed a wounded lieutenant and the sergeant who had brought the officer in, the sole survivors of their battalion. They told the Colonel that the Americans had virtually encircled the narrow strip of land still left under his command. Before they fled the two had seen the enemy beginning to roll up to the strongpoints in farmhouses to the rear. There there was a hill, the Lousberg, which dominated the whole of Aachen. Wilck knew what that meant. He turned to his surviving radio operator: 'Send this message: Request immediate artillery fire on House Sonne, House Landen and House Scheuer, plus Stockheide Mill.'

The operator knew what those orders meant. For the first time since the siege had started seven weeks earlier Wilck was bringing down artillery fire on his own positions, though he knew that those houses were still occupied by German troops. It was clear that the Colonel was prepared to go to any length to stop the American advance, even killing his own soldiers.

In one of those seemingly doomed positions, Otto Pesch, an ex-newspaper man recently invalided home from the Russian front, was watching the slow advance of the Americans on Schloss Rahe, once the home of Czar Alexander I on his annual visits to Aachen to take the waters and to gamble. Suddenly American dive-bombers fell out of the October sky and the bombs came whistling down. When he came up from the cellars later he found the kitchen in which he had been sitting covered in a mess of slimy cottage cheese. A bomb splinter had penetrated a huge churn of the stuff. Pesch's face turned white as he realized the narrowness of his escape.[*]

Half a mile away the first dust-covered Sherman of the 3rd Division's Task Force Hogan swept into the courtyard of Schloss Rahe. It bore the brightly coloured flag of the 'Lone Star' State, which was not surprising since it was the command tank of Lieutenant Colonel Sam 'Bill' Hogan from Texas. The castle was abandoned, but the signs of its former occupants were everywhere and it was evident that the mood of the vanished German defenders had been low. There were whisky bottles on all sides, unfortunately all empty.

Below, Wilck's men spotted the first enemy tanks. The Battle Commandant was informed and he promptly radioed Corps HQ: 'The Battle Group is defending itself stubbornly around the Lousberg against an enemy who is attacking from all sides now.' Then Wilck and his batman, Schulz, who had already packed the CO's bag, crawled out to see just how his defenders were getting on. They didn't stop for long; it was too dangerous. But as they returned Schulz saw tears in his chief's eyes. It had been all too much for him. The end was not far away now. Soon they'd need that bag.

[*] Pesch who was later to edit Germany's first postwar paper, *Die Aachener Nachrichten*.

25

SS *Obersturmführer* Rink was no fool, and he too realized that Aachen could not hold out much longer. Soon the last of the defenders would have to surrender, and Rink had determined that he was not going to be one of them. He had no intention of spending years in an Allied POW camp. He'd already guessed what his treatment would be as an officer of the *Waffen SS*, especially as a member of that elite division which bore the Führer's name. That afternoon he decided to start evacuating his wounded, prior to breaking out of the trapped garrison. The SS never abandoned their wounded.

For the task he had seven halftracks at his disposal, now parked seventy yards from his CP. He set a group of lightly wounded men to removing the mortars they contained and painting large red crosses on their sides. While that was being done, he assembled his handful of survivors and briefed them on the situation. Then he asked, 'Who can drive and knows Aachen? I need volunteers.'

Peter Schaaf didn't hesitate. He raised his hand and said he could drive and he was a local. Quickly eleven other SS troopers volunteered to try and break out before it was too late, including Schaaf's friend Willi Becker.

Rink nodded. 'All right; you move out at midnight. And as soon as you reach our lines, report by radio. I want to know the route you took.' Rink reasoned that if the halftracks could get through so could he, with the rest of his command, especially as they'd probably be on foot.

Midnight came. Aachen was sinking into a sea of flames which could be seen thirty miles away in Belgium. Above, American searchlights combed the skies for intruders, parting the clouds like ghostly fingers. To Peter Schaaf the very bricks seemed to glow red with the heat. Finally the halftracks were loaded and they were ready. Rink gave them their last instructions. He looked at Schaaf and Willi Becker in the lead halftrack packed with wounded SS men. 'All right, Schaaf, off you go. Best of luck.'

A moment later the halftracks disappeared into the darkness preparing to meet the first challenge of their ordeal, the Roermonderstrasse, the only road leading out of the area.

Schaaf put his foot down hard as he crouched behind the wheel. Despite the big red crosses painted on the side of the halftrack, he didn't trust the Yanks. At this time of the night they would be even more trigger-happy than normal. He prepared for the worst.

III

AIX-LA-CHAPELLE N'EXISTE PLUS

At last it was dawn and the final battle for Aachen was in full swing. In their bunker Wilck's staff officers, as nervous and as hollow-eyed as their men, started to hand out the daily ration of preludin tablets to help the weary defenders keep their eyes open. Outside, the attackers pressed closer. The men of the Big Red One had already lost 500 men in the last four days to add to the 3,000 casualties of their predecessors, the 30th Infantry Division. They wanted to get the job over with, but they were cautious and preferred to rely on armour, aerial bombardment and artillery to do the task for them. Still the infantry had to take the ground, cost what it may.

But the defenders' morale was breaking quickly. At the end of their tether, they succumbed to despair in their waterlogged foxholes and brick pits. Here and there they decided to make an end to it now – boot off, big toe curled round the trigger of a rifle, its muzzle stuck in the mouths, they blasted themselves into eternity. The misery and horror were over at last.

At about ten that morning Wilck received a useless signal from 81st Corps, signed General Koechling, the Corps Commander. It read: '81st Corps expresses its greatest admiration for the brave defenders of Aachen, fighting to the last for Folk and Führer.' It was the usual patriotic guff, intended more for outside consumption than for the defenders. All the same, Wilck, playing the propaganda game to the last, replied, 'Thank you. Expect enemy attacks soon all along our tight front. The defenders of Aachen are prepared for the final battle. Wilck.'

Soon thereafter Major Rink called briefly at Wilck's HQ. Before disappearing again, he asked the Battle Commandant if he had news of the arrival of his halftracks with the wounded men in the German lines. Wilck checked with 81st Corps HQ. Thirty minutes later their reply came back: 'Halftracks with wounded cannot be found. Signed Roems, Chief-of-Staff.'

Then *Obersturmführer* Rink of the Adolf Hitler Bodyguard disappeared from Aachen for good.

Schaaf, in the lead halftrack, had gone only a short distance down the Roermonderstrasse when an enemy machine gun opened up close by. Lead pattered on the sides of the vehicle like tropical rain on a tin roof. The wounded shouted and screamed, completely dependent as they were on their unwounded comrades. Schaaf kept his foot pressed down on the accelerator. Surely the Yanks could see his red crosses? Then, as abruptly as it had started, the firing ceased and the convoy rolled on through the empty streets. At a shattered café at one corner Schaaf, who of course knew Aachen intimately, swung to the right to lead the convoy through the tunnel that ran below the railway line. There they would be protected, for a few seconds at least, from enemy fire. One by one the halftracks followed his lead. Suddenly three civilians leapt out of a trench by the entrance to the tunnel. Recognizing the silver runes of the SS on Schaaf's collar, one of them yelled, 'The Americans are everywhere!'

'Don't worry old man,' Schaaf appeased the civilian. 'We're in touch with them. They know we're taking out the wounded. *Wiedersehen*, we've got to get on.'

The halftracks clattered through the tunnel, past wide-eyed civilians now coming out of the shadows by the score. A few minutes later they were out in the open once more and beginning the steep climb up the height which led out of Aachen.

But then their luck ran out. A Sherman tank loomed up out of nowhere and in a flash its electrically operated turret spun round and its 75mm cannon lined up Schaaf's vehicle. But then the turret flap was thrust open and a hand appeared and beckoned Schaaf to follow. Schaaf did as he was ordered and started to follow the tank, passing Sherman after Sherman of Hogan's task force, lined up carefully every four metres or so as if on parade. Schaaf looked at Becker. They hadn't had a chance from the start and now they were heading for the PoW cage. He knew he was right when an officer stopped him and cried the traditional words in German, '*Für Dich ist der Krieg aus*' (For you the war is over). It was.

At about the same time Wilck advised 81st Corps HQ, 'All ammo gone after severe house-to-house fighting. No water and no food. Enemy close to command post of the last defenders of the Imperial City. Radio prepared for destruction.'

The reply came: 'Long live the defenders of Aachen!'

Soon after that Wilck sent off his final signal: 'We're reporting out. Best wishes to our comrades and our loved ones.'

Just before Wilck ordered his radio destroyed, the Colonel's former Division managed to radio him: 'The 246th People's Grenadier Division expresses its gratitude and admiration for the effort and courage of its comrades. We salute you.'

Right to the very end the troops were playing the game that Dr Josef Goebbels, the Reich Propaganda Minister and Minister for Public Enlightenment, had mapped out for them – heroes all, fighting to the last bullet and the last man.

Five minutes later the bunker signaller destroyed the one remaining radio and Aachen was cut off from the outside world. In the far distance the defenders could hear the familiar sound of German 88mm cannon and knew that meant that their own 81st Corps were bombarding the American positions surrounding them. The German High Command had given them up.

Now Wilck no longer needed to fear Rink, whom he knew had been planted on the garrison to make them fight to the last – or else.

Rink had vanished. Where, Wilck didn't know or care. All he knew was that he had to make that overwhelming decision which he had known he would have to make all along. It would be his fatal duty to surrender one of Germany's great Imperial cities where thirty-two German Emperors and Kings had been crowned since the time of Charlemagne. Aachen was a symbol of German nationalism, part of the National Socialist mythology. It was also Germany's premier Catholic city, many of whose citizens had opposed the godless Nazis and suffered for it.

Wilck also had to consider his family. What would happen to them if he surrendered? All 'battle commandants' in charge of important German cities had been forced to sign an undertaking by the Gestapo acknowledging that if they didn't do their utmost to defend their city, they realized that their next-of-kin could be shot or sent to a concentration camp. Years later, aged 80 and spending his declining years not far from Aachen, ex-Colonel Wilck recalled, 'It was the most difficult decision of my whole life. But in the end I decided to surrender, though as a professional soldier I had always regarded the act of surrender with the greatest disgust.'

But now he made that decision and was immediately faced by a new problem. How was he going to do it? Already two German officers attempting to surrender had been shot by the Americans, although they had carried a makeshift white flag. It wasn't surprising. Outside, in the smoking ruins of Aachen, all was confusion. In the end he decided to ask for volunteers from among the thirty-odd prisoners from the Big Red One whom he held in the HQ bunker and two of them agreed to go – Sergeant Ewart Padgett and Pfc James Haswell.

A white flag was found, a German officer wished them good luck in English, the door to the bunker was forced open and, taking a deep breath, the two ex-prisoners stepped cautiously into the open. Almost at once bullets came whizzing their way. Furiously they waved the white flag, then staggered forward over the rubble to a house occupied by American infantry. Suspiciously a scruffy rifleman leaned out of the glassless window and waved them forward. Sergeant Padgett turned and signalled to the German officer who was accompanying them at some distance. Minutes later they were behind American lines, relating their news to the first US officer they chanced upon. Two hours later they entered the bunker once more and reported that the American command was prepared to talk with Wilck. He had made contact.

By ten o'clock that morning Colonel Wilck had shaved and put on a well-brushed uniform. With him he carried his suitcase, already neatly packed, but he was without his service pistol. Sergeant Padgett had nicked that before he left!

A young American officer exchanged a few words with him before leading him to the only surviving house in the Hansemannsplatz, now the HQ of Colonel Corley. Through an interpreter, Corley told him that the Germans had treated their American prisoners in a decent fashion and that the Americans would do the same and generally abide by the Geneva Convention. He then asked for Wilck's pistol. Politely the Colonel was informed that Sergeant Padgett had beaten him to it.

At that moment a jeep stopped outside in which were Wilck's batman, Schulz, an American driver and one of Wilck's battalion commanders, a Major Heimann. Corley asked one more question: had Wilck laid any mines in the area of the bunker? Wilck said he had not and then asked if he could speak to the hundreds of Germans now being formed up to march to the POW cages, to which Corley agreed.

It was standard stuff which the Allies would hear often enough in the months to come. He had surrendered because the defence had become hopeless. He had no desire to sacrifice any further German lives to no purpose. He wished his men the best of luck and was then driven off to spend the next three years behind barbed wire in a cage just outside London. *

It was exactly five minutes to twelve on Saturday, 21 October, 1944. The six-week Battle of Aachen was over. Across the border the Belgian daily *La Nation* headlined the surrender with the words '*Aix-la-Chapelle n'existe plus*'.

* Rink and his handful of men survived. They escaped dressed as nuns!

IV

WE MUST MAINTAIN THE ILLUSION THAT THE US ARMY CANNOT BE BEATEN

One month before Aachen surrendered, General Bradley, commander of the US 12th Army Group, had told Patton, Commander of his 3rd Army, that the siege and final capture of the port of Brest in September, 1944, had been too costly for the US Army. In the end it had taken three divisions and they had suffered just short of 10,000 casualties. As Patton noted the exchange in his diary, 'I would not say this to anyone but you, and I have given different excuses to my staff and higher echelons, but we must take Brest in order to maintain the illusion that the US Army cannot be beaten.'

But once Brest had been taken, the other French fortresses held by the Germans were left to wither on the vine, with no effort being made to capture them. Indeed half a dozen French coastal strongholds held out until the end of the war, when the US Army was in the heart of the Reich. One of them, Lorient, didn't give in till four days *after* the official surrender of all German Forces in Europe. It did so on 12 May, 1944, when Lorient's quartermaster made his daily report to the city's Battle Commandant, General Frambacher, that there were no more railway sleepers available to be made into sawdust and mixed with the daily flour ration for bread-making. Without their bread ration, General Farmbacher knew that his men couldn't be expected to fight, so he duly surrendered.

The capture of Aachen had not been as costly as that of Brest, but it had been costly enough, and time-consuming. It had taken three experienced divisions (the 30th, the 1st Infantry and the 3rd Armoured) to capture it and the 30th, which had seen the brunt of the fighting, had suffered 3,000 casualties, or one-fifth of its strength. About sixty American tanks were lost in the street fighting.

Now, as Hitler's prophecy, with its ironic truth, was being posted everywhere in the ruins of Aachen by the victorious Americans – 'Give me five years and you will not recognize Germany again' – the US High Command debated what they should do about other fortified German cities which stood in the way of their advance into the heart of the Third Reich.

Some thought they should be circumvented and left to starve, especially as the US Army no longer possessed the specialist troops needed to tackle heavily fortified German positions. D-Day and the Battle for Normandy had taken the lives of too many trained engineers specializing in attacks on bunkers and pillboxes. Flame-throwers and their operators, plus the specialist armoured troops used in such operations, were in short supply. More often than not the Americans had to go cap-in-hand to the British to borrow 'Churchill's funnies' – flails for exploding mines, flame-throwing tanks, bridge-laying armoured vehicles and the like. The US Army didn't possess such things. Bradley had declined them even before Normandy, dismissing them as not of American make.

Some, however, like Bradley, thought that the attacks into the Reich ought to be continued even though Hitler's Empire looked as if it might collapse at any moment. It was a matter of prestige, an attitude that was, at first at least, unwittingly promoted by General Eisenhower.

By the end of September, 1944, it was clear that Montgomery's 'knife-like thrust' from Arnhem into the German Ruhr and then on to Berlin itself had failed. Now, with more and more American troops pouring into Europe from the States, Eisenhower was faced with the quandary of what to do with them. In the end he evolved his so-called 'broad front strategy', which entailed piling up army after army, six of them spread out over four hundred miles or more and all commanded by ambitious generals. Naturally these generals were concerned about the prestige of the US Army. But there was also the matter of personal prestige. Without battles and great campaigns fought and won, they might well yet retire into slippered obscurity.

Indeed General Patton, the commander of the US 3rd Army down in French Lorraine, had already got himself involved in the battle for yet another frontier fortress, that of Metz. In the end it would take him three months, two corps and thousands of casualties to capture the city, which had no vital strategic value whatsoever. Still, its capture was a matter of prestige, both that of the US 3rd Army and, naturally, that of George S. Patton Jnr.

A few of the less ambitious and more complacent generals thought that after the German Army had been destroyed in France there would be no need for attacks into the Reich. Germany was obviously on the verge of collapse. Most of the pundits, especially those not engaged at the sharp end and not paying the butcher's bill, thought that Hitler's 1,000 Year Reich would probably not last until Christmas.

Both the Supreme Commander and Montgomery thought this likely, even though the Germans had given Monty a very bloody nose at Arnhem. So why bother so much about operations in Germany, where probably at this very moment every major city was being turned into a fortress? As the newspapers back home were confidently proclaiming, they'd be 'bringing the boys back home for Christmas'.

But the Führer had other ideas altogether.

On that same afternoon when Colonel Wilck surrendered Aachen to the Americans, far away at the Führer's HQ, deep in the heart of an East Prussian forest, Hitler received the man Allied Intelligence called 'the most dangerous man in Europe', *Obersturmbannführer* Otto Skorzeny, the head of the German equivalent of the SAS. The year before, he had seized the Italian dictator Mussolini from his mountain-top prison. Now he had come to report on his latest daring exploit – the kidnapping of the son of Admiral Horthy, by which he had kept the Hungarian dictator on the side of Germany in her battle against Soviet Russia.

Hitler looked up at the sabre-scarred face of his visitor and said, 'Well done. I am promoting you and awarding you the

German Cross in Gold. Now tell me about Operation Mickey Mouse' (the code name for the Hungarian operation).

Skorzeny described the kidnapping and told how he had smuggled him out of the Hungarian castle rolled up in a carpet.

When Skorzeny rose to leave Hitler held him back, saying, 'Don't go for a minute. I have another job for you, perhaps the most important of your life. So far a very few people know of the plan in which you have a great part to play. In December Germany will start a great offensive which may well decide her fate.'

Hitler then briefly outlined his new plan, code-named '*die Wacht am Rhein*' (the Watch on the Rhine) to fool the Allies, if they found out about it, into thinking that it was a defensive operation in the Rhineland. Hitler explained to Skorzeny that the Western Allies thought Germany prostrate, almost dead. But what if the 'corpse' should rise again and strike them such a crushing blow in the West that the British and Americans would be forced to sue for an armistice favourable to Germany? To emphasize his point, the Führer detailed the huge force he had been building up during the autumn.

'I'm telling you this,' he continued, 'so that you realize that nothing has been forgotten. Now, one of the most important tasks in the offensive will be entrusted to you.'

That afternoon, while Dr Goebbels pondered gloomily over how he might present the depressing news of the fall of Aachen to the German people, *Obersturmbannführer* Skorzeny flew back to his own HQ, feeling happier than he had done for many a day. Thanks to the stubborn defence of Aachen, Germany was in a position to go on the offensive once again, perhaps even win the war after all. For Hitler had also told him that all sorts of devastating 'wonder weapons' would be ready by the time of the great attack.

Naturally the Western Allies knew nothing of Hitler's project, though with the Intelligence facilities at their disposal, including the Bletchley decoding operation, they should have done. But that autumn the Allied Top Brass believed what they wanted to believe. Aachen had admittedly been a bit of a shock for them, when they had thought that Germany was finished after the destruction of the *Wehrmacht* in France the previous summer. But as they now prepared to push deeper into the Reich, they regarded Aachen as little more than an unfortunate hiccup. They were wrong, disastrously so. Within two months whole US divisions would be surrendering and others would be broken reeds, having suffered hundreds, even thousands, of casualties. It would be nearly six months before the Allies were faced with the prospect of attacking another major German fortified position such as Aachen, and by then many of the young soldiers who now thought the war was over bar the shouting would be dead, wounded or behind the wire in German prison cages – 150,000 of them.

TWO

OCTOBER, 1944 – MARCH, 1945

I

WHAT NEWS FROM TWELVELAND?

For September the night was unseasonably cold. The chill wind, sweeping across the runway of the remote RAF field, seemed to be coming straight from Siberia. Standing on the tarmac not far from the Halifax, being readied for its flight into enemy territory on the other side of the Channel, the little crowd of British and American officers and a handful of civilians turned up the collars of their overcoats and prayed that it would soon be over and they could return to the RAF mess for a stiff drink. The mess had long been closed but at times like this there was always plenty of drink about. The men who were going and those who had been responsible for getting them ready were certainly ready for a drink. For this was a special occasion. Spies and agents had flown from this field many times in the preceding years, but they had usually been dropped over territory where they could expect a friendly welcome from the local underground. This time the man who was soon to leave was very different. He was flying to Germany and, if he were met at all, it would probably be by the *Geheime Staatspolizei*, the Gestapo.

The agent waddled over to the plane in his heavy gear, carrying his flight helmet in his hand, accompanied by an officer who spoke with an American accent. Introductions were made to the RAF crew; then the man with the American accent helped to push the bulky figure of the agent into the plane's belly hatch.

The pilot disappeared behind his controls. The engines started to turn. The props sliced the night air. The spectators stepped back out of the propellor wash. The plane started to vibrate and tremble as the pilot increased the revs. Over at the blacked-out control tower a green light began flashing. It was the signal to go. The pilot pushed forward on the throttle and released the brakes. The Halifax rolled on to the runway, its wingtip lights on now. Flares shot up ahead and the plane began to rise from the ground. A few moments later it was airborne. The first attempt by the American OSS, the wartime forerunner of the CIA, to parachute an agent into Nazi Germany was under way.

Back in early 1940, before Germany marched westwards, the Gestapo started to round up the widespread British spy network inside the Reich. Unfortunately, when the two leading SIS agents on the Continent, Stevens and Best, were caught at Venlo in Holland in 1939 they were carrying with them details of all their other agents, who were then picked up with no difficulty, leaving SIS HQ in Queen Anne Gate totally blind in the Reich. As Winston Churchill complained, 'with a telescope I can read the time on the clock tower at Calais from Dover, but that's about all I know of what is going on in Europe now.'

For nearly three years thereafter Britain, and later America, was without agents inside Germany, apart from a few neutrals, though when it started to become obvious that Germany was losing the war a couple of German turncoats began to deliver information to the OSS chiefs in Berne in return for special privileges after the war. Ultra had filled some of the gaps, but it could tell Allied Intelligence little about the mood and morale of the German people and what their reaction would be when the Allies finally invaded their country. Would they fight for every large city, for instance? Did they intend to undertake the same kind of 'scorched earth' policy as the Russians had done in 1941/42? Many questions with few answers.

However, by 1944, there *were* native-born Germans who were prepared to chance their lives against the Gestapo and parachute into what was now hostile country. Some were political refugees who had lived abroad since the thirties and bitterly hated the Nazis who had driven them from their homeland. Others were newly captured soldiers who felt they had been betrayed by Hitler and were prepared to do something about it. And some were simply young adventurers who would do anything to escape from the overwhelming boredom, and lack of sex, in the POW camps.

The first OSS agent to go was Jupp Kappius, a working-class socialist who had been forced to flee Germany in 1937 and was now on the Gestapo's death list. Trained and outfitted by the Americans in London, Kappius now prepared for his drop near the small town of Soegel. He remembered the myriad instructions given to him by the OSS officers at their headquarters in Grosvenor Street – how he should avoid any parachute strap marks on his shoulders and thighs, the first things the Gestapo looked for; how to jump straight, hands and chin well tucked in, otherwise he'd get a nasty bruise on his chin which again would give him away.

Two hours out of England the dispatcher waddled down the fuselage and yelled, 'Running in!' The engines began to throttle back. They were loosing speed. Then the green light glowed. The dispatcher slapped him across the shoulder and shouted, 'Go!' Next moment Kappius was through the hole and falling into the night. Above him the canopy billowed out and he started to float gently downwards. Moments later he hit the furrows of a ploughed field in what appeared to be the middle of nowhere. It was just after midnight on 2 September, 1944. America's first agent to drop into the Third Reich had landed.

Two months later the OSS in London and Washington perfected a radio device which would make the lives of the agents now parachuting into the Reich in ever-increasing numbers much easier and safer, and one that could help to thwart the German *Peildienst* (literally 'sound service') which seemed to operate in every sizeable German town. One of the agents' most dangerous tasks was signalling back to London whatever they had discovered. This meant finding a safe place where a radio set and aerial could be established. But even using high-speed morse it was hard to reduce the length of time needed to less than half an hour, long enough for the local German radio detection HQ to home in on the signal. The radio detection vans would take to the streets, their roof aerials twitching back and forth while the operator tried to find the exact place from where the enemy signal was coming.

To remove this danger, the OSS had developed a transmitter-receiver small enough to be easily concealed by the agent. Signals coming from this battery-powered radio were picked up by an aeroplane carrying a machine which could record the exchange between the agent and his aerial contact on a spool of wire.

The inventor of the device called it 'Jean-Eleanor', after two American women he admired, the 'Jean' component being carried by the agent, while the 'Eleanor' was installed in the fast British fighter, the Mosquito. These unorthodox planes flew from the RAF station at Watton in East Anglia and thereby direct contact could be made between the agent and the controller in the aircraft. Now for the first time vital information could be passed to and from the field under active service conditions in a matter of hours or less.

While the OSS and a somewhat reluctant British SOE (OSS penetrations of the Third Reich still remain secret*) sent more and more agents into Germany, two large mother organizations were being built up in those parts of Germany over which the Western Allies would probably fight once they had crossed the Rhine.

Moving into Southern Germany from Austria, a large mixed German-Austrian-American OSS mission, under the leadership of the future Austrian publisher Ernst Molden, crossed the Alps, set up shop in Munich and penetrated as far west as Regensburg. In other words, the agent network, aided by a handful of probably turncoat Austrians and Germans who called themselves 'the Resistance', would eventually lie across the route to be taken by Patton's 3rd Army when Eisenhower ordered it to change direction and deal with the supposed 'Alpine Redoubt'.

Meanwhile Jupp Kappius set up his headquarters in the Ruhr in the industrial city of Bochum at 15 Burgstrasse. Here, in a building that provided the ideal cover – a wholesale kitchen supply business, run by fellow socialist conspirators – Kappius

* When, some years ago, the present author attempted to find out the whereabouts of a senior German agent from the Nazi Foreign Ministry who reported directly to OSS chief Allen Dulles in Switzerland, he encountered a blank. Even the considerable assistance of a German government minister did not ease the process. It seemed that the agent in question, Fritz Kolbe, had disappeared without trace in 1945 – something which was hardly likely.

spread his tentacles far and wide. His contacts ranged from factory workers and miners to managers and, in one case, a town police chief.

Many of his contacts, especially the communists, were prepared to take part in an armed rising against the State when the time came. They had already armed themselves from the munitions factories of the Ruhr, but Kappius, with that single-mindedness which kept him alive until the end of the war, wanted more weapons parachuted in before the rising began. So he sent his wife, who had already joined him disguised as a Red Cross nurse tending wounded soldiers from Austria, back along the same route to arrange an arms drop. But nothing came of it, like most of his immediate plans, save for individual acts of sabotage in the Ruhr factories.

Nevertheless Kappius and Molden were able to study the people they had come to rescue from the Nazis. What struck them was the normality of the life around them. The factories and mines still operated despite years of Allied bombing. The hundreds of thousands of Ruhr workers who had been called up for the Armed Forces had been replaced by foreign labour, forced or otherwise, which carried out its duties loyally under the eagle eye of the Gestapo and the police.

Trains ran on time. Post and newspapers were delivered punctually. Rations were regular, but short. And, as in so many other spheres of life in wartime Germany, the local black market made up for the deficiencies. Although many had been bombed out three or four times, the civilians appeared to Kappius to be better-dressed than Londoners.

Naturally such matters of morale interested his spymasters back in London and, as the Battle of the Bulge drew to a close in January, 1945, the masters of the war in the shadows were vitally interested in the determination of the local citizens to fight on. Would the Germans turn the many Ruhr cities into other versions of Aachen, arm the civilians and force the Allies to fight city by city all the way to Berlin?

For the Allied camp was now flooded with rumours, mainly originating (on Goebbels' orders) in supposedly neutral Switzerland, that diehard Nazis were building a great last-ditch fortress, the 'National Redoubt', in the Alps of Austria and

Germany and memories of the obstinate defence of Aachen the previous autumn came to mind. As the planners at Eisenhower's headquarters in Paris made their final decisions on the Allied crossing of the Rhine, they began to wonder what faced them on the other side. The fight seemed to have gone out of the defenders of the western bank of the river, but what was the situation on the eastern bank, especially in the Ruhr?

The same questions were being asked about the great Munich, Augsburg, Stuttgart industrial complex in the south, now being spied on by Molden's mixed bag of Austrians, Germans, Americans and deserters from the *Wehrmacht*. To reach the National Redoubt, if it existed, the American 3rd and 7th Armies would have to pass through that area. But what provision, if any, had the Germans made for defending it?

While the frustrated Allied Intelligence officers at Eisenhower's HQ tried to find the answers to these questions from within Germany, the veterans of the long War of Twelveland* tried to influence events from without.

For soon Montgomery would begin his crossing of the Rhine and would need all the help he could get. In particular, the fewer enemy troops who faced him the better his chance of success. So now, working independently of the SOE and its agents *in situ*, who were not in any case producing much which would influence the battle to come, the SIS went to work.

---

* The SIS codename for Germany. Each country had a number, used by the spymasters at SIS's London HQ in Queen Anne's Gate. It *was* known to the Germans, but apparently never changed.

II

DOUBLE CROSS

Officially it was called the 'Twenty Committee'. Unofficially the cynical veterans of the SIS and its domestic counterpart MI 5 called it the 'Double Cross Committee', a play on the Roman numeral for twenty. But in essence the name gave away its real purpose, which was to turn every German agent who arrived in Britain during the war. A couple of hangings of German spies at Pentonville at the outset of the war soon convinced those who were to follow, mostly non-Germans, which choice they would make if offered it: hang or work for us.

In September, 1940, with British fortunes at their lowest, Snow, as the German agent was code-named, made his first attempt to contact his German control, Major Ritter, in Hamburg.* He did so by radio, operating the set from, of all places, a dingy cell in London's Wandsworth Prison.

Thereafter a whole string of German agents were turned and started telling the *Abwehr* in a remote turn-of-the-century villa just outside Hamburg (it's still there) what the officers of the Double Cross Committee wanted them to know. Year in, year out they worked for the British until the *Abwehr* believed that they had a huge spy organization inside the United Kingdom, ranging from Welsh Nationalist dockers to officers on the staff of Bradley's HQ. By 1944 they had become the mainstay of the great British pre-D-Day deception scheme, the purpose of which

---

* Snow was a Welshman who had worked as agent for the British before the war in Germany as a travelling salesman. But his cover had been blown by Ritter and he had succumbed to bribes of money and women to work for the Nazis. In essence Snow was not only a double agent, but a *triple one* too.

was to fool the Germans as to where the Allies would land on the Continent. Hitler showered them with gifts of money, letters of praise and even, in several cases, coveted Iron Crosses for the information they passed, at the risk of their lives, to German Intelligence. It might just as well have been that their British controls could have awarded them the MBE or some such for the sterling work they were doing for the British cause. Instead they got an increased meat ration and, if they were lucky, the services of a whore now and again.

But by the end of 1944 it seemed as if the double-cross agents had virtually outlived their usefulness. Admittedly they still had a rôle to play in the last great Allied deception – the attempt to fool the Germans into keeping large numbers of troops in Norway in case, as Hitler personally believed, Churchill would pick another soft option, as was his wont, and attack that country. But when British POWs revealed to the Germans that they belonged to the 52nd Lowland Division,* which the former knew had been earmarked specially for the invasion of Norway, the attempt to keep up the Norwegian deception seemed futile.

In early November, 1944, when it became known to the Double Cross Committee that Montgomery intended to cross the Lower Rhine in force, the Intelligence planners decided that there was room for yet another deception operation. The plan was to detain as many German troops as possible in Northern Germany, Norway and Denmark, so that they couldn't oppose Monty's on the Rhine.

Well before Montgomery was ready, the Germans received the first information from one of their 'V-Mann', as they were called, who reported that he had heard in the Norfolk area that the Allies were preparing for an airborne and seaborne landing at the mouth of the River Ems, or perhaps in Holland. This startling information was rushed straight to Hitler, who couldn't make up his mind whether to take it seriously or not. But the 'Admiral in Charge of the German Bay' did. He ordered precious troops from both the Army and Navy to be concentrated in those

* The 52nd Divison became earmarked as a 'mountain division', the only one in the British Army, in early 1941. Thereafter it trained as such for nearly four years, only to take part in its first action in the lowest part of Europe – Holland!

areas. The Double Cross Committee had sown the first seeds of doubt.

Although the German High Command possessed the 'Eclipse' papers and were not therefore convinced that there was any danger of a landing on the North Sea coast, Hitler started to change his mind. Given the Allies' superiority on land and sea, he thought it possible that they might well chance a kind of second mini-D Day.

His change of mind was strengthened by another report from one of the Double Cross agents that the British 1st Airborne Division, which had been shattered the previous September at Arnhem, had now been reformed in Lincolnshire. From what the 'V-Mann' had been able to find out, the new First Airborne was intended for a landing at the North Sea port of Emden. At the same time a seaborne operation would begin.

Hitler's fears were heightened by the news the next day that during the night there had been a particularly heavy RAF raid on Wilhelmshaven, the most important naval base of the *Kriegsmarine*. The raid was completely out of character at this time when 'Bomber' Harris, the chief of the RAF Bomber Command, was concentrating all his efforts on the bombing of the immediate area along the Rhine where the Germans suspected Montgomery would try to cross. Even the sceptical German High Command now started to come round to the Führer's was of thinking. Perhaps there *was* going to be an Allied invasion of the German North Sea coast three hundred miles from the Rhine.

The whole German fleet of small ships, including torpedo boats and submarines patrolling the North Sea, were ordered to be on the lookout for enemy activity between the Wash and the Humber. Night reconnaissance flights by the surviving German Junkers 88 night-fighters were also ordered. But German sea and air reconnaissance was hampered by British command of the entire area. Hardly a plane was able to infiltrate British air space and the seaborne forces fared no better, as the exits to their harbours had been mined.

All the same, although they knew only of the enemy's intentions from these 'V-Männer', most of whom had left Germany years before to drop into Britain by parachute, the Germans continued to take the matter seriously. Montgomery's attack on the Rhine grew ever nearer, the North German Naval Command hectically prepared emergency counter-measures. U-boat crews without subs, crews of heavier ships which hadn't dared to go to sea for years, marines who hadn't seen action since the invasion of Norway back in 1940, in fact anyone in the German North Sea naval districts who could carry and fire a rifle, were formed into battle groups, alarm battalions, marine divisions, and so on. The overall commander of the North Sea area, *Generalfeldmarschall* Ernst Busch, now ordered General Siegfried Rasp, until recently Himmler's chief-of-staff, to combine all these disparate units into *Korps Ems* – not a particularly strong unit, consisting only of two weak infantry divisions, the newly formed 2nd Marine Division, some armour and two training battalions of the SS.

All the same the cultivated gentlemen of the Double Cross Committee were very pleased with themselves. They had drawn off a whole new corps, handily placed for sending to the Rhine and making Montgomery's task more difficult. Their last deception operation of the Second World War had been a complete success.

But as the third week of March, 1945, approached and it needed only a matters of hours before Montgomery attacked – and, unknown to the latter, General Patton as well – they would not have been so happy had they realized that they had created a double-edged weapon. For that *Korps Ems* would prove a thorn in Monty's flesh that would irritate him almost to the end of the war.

It was a crazy time, this late March of 1945. The British called it 'swanning', the American 'the rat race'. Both meant that Allied armour had almost a free run in the immediate vicinity of the eastern bank of the newly crossed Rhine. The Shermans and the new US Pershing tanks, which were replacing the former, no longer fanned out over the countryside as they had done during the two months of fighting on the western side. They by-passed the towns and villages, leaving the infantry to mop up behind them. And if the infantry couldn't do it without severe casualties, the feared *jabos* of the TAC Air Force or artillery

50

were whistled up to blast the reluctant Germans to pieces. If innocent civilians got hurt in the bombardment, then it was just 'tough titty'.

For Patch's tankers of his US 7th Army, men of the 10th, 12th, 14th Armored Divisions and the veteran 6th Armored, this type of warfare involved the reconnaissance elements crawling forward, 'daring' the German to reveal his position by firing at them. At the point of the armoured division, which could stretch as much as 20 miles behind it, there would be a lone tank or armoured car. It would be linked by radio to another one half a mile behind, which in its turn was in visual contact with the armoured infantry in their halftracks a little further back. Sooner or later the unfortunate men at point would run into a roadblock covered by mines, machine guns and the lethal *panzerfausts*, wielded by teenage fanatics of the Hitler Youth.

Then the fun would start and the men at the point would die. Immediately, the second tanks would alert the armoured infantry. While the tank blasted away at the road block, the infantrymen would hurry up in their halftracks, jump over the steel sides of their vehicles and fan out to left and right for their assault on the roadblock.

As the BBC Correspondent attached to General Patch's US 7th Army commented on one such encounter with typical British understatement, 'Being in the lead tank is one of the war's most uncomfortable jobs'. He might have added, 'And one of the most lethal too.'

All the same the rat race was a happy time for those involved. Senior officers found that control had become a headache and they often lost contact with their smaller units. Previously the men had mostly fought and lived in empty countryside, their bed for the night a shattered barn or a hole in the ground. Now they were in populous villages and towns, mixing for the first time with the enemy. They did just as they pleased. They were no longer 'liberators', they were 'conquerors'. And the only controls were in the hands of junior officers and NCOs.

As US General Franklin Davis, then a combat major, wrote long afterwards: 'There were new benefits to being victors . . . They often slept in houses, apartments, taverns, hotels, even sumptuous villas. Once a town fell to them, their billeting parties had only to select a good spot, tell the German inhabitants "*raus*" and they were in.'

The non-fraternization ban was not taken very seriously, even by generals. As Patton once declared, 'As long as my GIs keep their helmets on and their feet on the ground, it's not fraternization – it's fornication.' But then 'Ole Blood an' Guts' had always believed that 'a man who won't fuck, won't fight.' And sometimes when a 'frowlin' wouldn't 'make out' voluntarily, she was forced. Cases of rape brought to trial mounted steadily that March, and in Paris a worried Eisenhower considered reintroducing the death sentence for that offence.

That last week of March everything seemed too easy. It was wine, women and song all the way. On the last day of the month elements of the US 63rd Division moved into Old Heidelberg, one of them singing a song he had learned at his mother's knee: 'Oh Heidelberg, dear Heidelberg. Thy name we'll never forget. That golden haze of student days will live with us yet.'

Although the city housed 30,000 German military wounded, Hitler had not allowed it to declare itself an 'open city'. But its citizens no longer had any desire to die for a cause which was already clearly lost. They negotiated a surrender with the Americans who advanced through the university city doing a little sightseeing and a lot of drinking. They saw the historic red sandstone castle, destroyed in the 17th century by the French, but still with its huge wine barrel which was reputed to hold fifty thousand gallons of wine. Unfortunately the barrel was empty, but a rumour spread that up the road at Neckargemünd was a huge warehouse full of cases of champagne. Soon the eager GIs of the 1st Battalion, 253rd Infantry, were declaring the champagne 'the best lemon soda pop' they had ever drunk.

That night the 862nd Field Artillery Battalion heard about the Neckargemünd warehouse and were soon filling up an ammunition trailer with bottle after bottle of the finest French champagne before rolling on to their next position. But en route the convoy was fired on by the Germans and unfortunately one shell struck the trailer carrying the champagne. Those in the convoy who didn't know the trailer contained booze and not shells instinctively ducked for cover and waited for the explosion to come. It didn't! Instead, as the Division History records,

52

there was 'a gigantic mound of foam and froth which served to mark the previous location of the trailer.' The Battalion went dry that night.

Thereafter the Commanding General, General Hibbs, decreed, as the 63rd moved out of Heidelberg to make way for the 'canteen commandos' of the rear echelon, that every officer in the division should receive two bottles of champagne and every enlisted man one.

Shortly thereafter Division Headquarters moved out of the city, heading for nearby Aglasterhausen. The 63rd Divisional History records: 'The route to Aglasterhausen, where the Division was next headquartered, was clearly marked by empty champagne bottles along the side of the road.'

So for a few days at the end of March the fighting men enjoyed the fruits of their victory on the Rhine. The 'nervous Nellies' had seemingly been proved wrong. Resistance had been only sporadic. Nowhere had the Germans put up a really spirited defence. Admittedly the Americans had yet to tackle a German town of any tactical or strategic importance. Nevertheless Aachen and its bitter seven-week defence by the Germans was all but forgotten. Now it was going to be 'frowleins', lemon soda pop and loot all the way. But, unfortunately for the advancing US 3rd and 7th Armies heading for the supposed Alpine Redoubt, it was not going to be like that at all. Serious trouble loomed ahead, and to those who knew the volatile character of General Patton, Commander of the 3rd Army, it came as no surprise that he would be the one to encounter it first. To his cost he would be the first to discover that the Germans, admittedly, beaten on the Rhine, were not going to give up as easily as had been anticipated. Patton's Army was going to suffer its first defeat since the previous December.

III

THAT GUY DESERVES A
CONGRESSIONAL MEDAL

On the afternoon of 26 March Captain Abraham Baum, a former
pattern cutter in a Bronx ladies' blouse factory and now S-2 of
the Fourth Armored Division's 10th Armored Infantry, was
dozing in the sun on the bonnet of a halftrack. By now he had
nine months of combat experience behind him and was a typical
Fourth Division man, 'full of piss and vinegar', as someone said
of the men of Patton's favourite division.

The son of strict Jewish parents, he had been appalled by
Patton's profanity when he first addressed the Division. Now he
was cocksure and aggressive, with a chestful of medals for
bravery and the nickname of 'Able' which summed up his un-
questionable military prowess.

At two o'clock that afternoon he was shaken awake by a lieutenant who answered his grumpy, 'What the hell is it?' with,
'Able, you're wanted at headquarters. The Old Man wants to
speak to you.'

Minutes later Baum was facing Colonel Creighton Abrams,
Commander of the Fourth's Combat Command B, who one day
would be Commander-in-Chief of the ill-fated US Army in
Vietnam. Abrams wasted no words: 'We have a special mission
for you. Orders directly from General Patton. You know where
Hammelburg is?'

'Yessir,' Baum answered. 'It's about sixty miles from here.'

Abrams nodded. 'Yes, and there's a prisoner-of-war camp at
Hammelburg. We want you to take a task force and liberate as
many Americans as you can. We think there are about three

54

hundred officers in the *Oflag*.' The Colonel hesitated and seemed embarrassed. Then, 'The Division is not to follow you. You'll be on your own. We'll give you the best we have available. You've got to get back to us whichever way you can. You understand?'

Baum forced a smile and, turning to his Battalion Commander, Colonel Cohen, he said, 'This is no way to get rid of me. I'll be back.' He wouldn't.

Abrams and Cohen then briefed Baum on his mission. In all he would take with him nearly four hundred men, divided among the tankers of the 37th Tank Battalion and the infantry of the 10th Armored. All would be motorized and, as there would be elements of two German divisions at least facing the task force, Baum was ordered to take side roads, avoiding towns. Hammelburg was to be taken, the prisoners 'snatched' and Baum Force make its way back in any way its commander thought suitable. The round trip would take them some 120 miles into enemy territory and Baum was not surprised when, as he left, he heard Abrams declare, 'If this mission is accomplished, that guy deserves a Congressional Medal of Honor'. But it didn't encourage him much when he recalled that most winners of America's top award for bravery usually received it posthumously!

The breakout began at nine o'clock that night. After a brief artillery bombardment the task force headed for the village of Schweinheim, where it would, according to the plan, break through the thin crust of the German defences and then roll on, hopefully unhindered. That wasn't to be. Almost as soon as the tanks started to move the darkness was lit by the scarlet flame of a rocket. The Germans had spotted them and were firing their dreaded *panzerfausts*. That lone rocket seemed to act as a signal. Long bursts of Spandau hissed towards the Americans and flights of tracer splattered the decks of the advancing tanks.

The Americans reacted fast. The infantry ran forward, firing from the hip as they went. A Sherman was hit. The tank commander and his crew bailed out in panic. Giving vent to his rage in a stream of curses that would have shocked his orthodox parents back in the States, Baum called up the NCO in charge of the next Sherman in the column and ordered, 'Get that fucking thing out of the way.'

Once again the tanks started to advance through the village. Scarlet flame stabbed the darkness on all sides. On the ground the panting infantry ran from house to house silencing the German positions, expecting and giving no quarter. But still Baum was in serious trouble. Corporal William Smith, who was there that night, recalled, 'Our platoon moved in to clear the left side. The platoon leader's tank was hit and it blocked the street. And the Krauts slipped in back of us and hit our rear tank with bazookas. We were trapped and I began to sweat.'

But the infantry swept forward once more and the driver of the lead tank discovered that it could still move, but only in reverse. He flung back the gear shift and sped back the way they had come.

Now the opposition was beginning to weaken. Baum's vehicles worked their way through the village as the men on the decks, tensed and expectant, fired to left and right.

By two-thirty that morning they were on their way once more through the silent countryside. They passed through the next five enemy villages without a single shot being fired at them. Apparently they had caught the Germans by surprise. They skirted the city of Aschaffenburg and headed on a secondary road for the small town of Lohr. Baum now felt that he was going to make it to Hammelburg after all. He urged greater speed, hoping that he would be able to keep the Germans off balance.

As the first light softened the sky the men of the Task Force could see the houses of Lohr and Baum's light tanks took the lead. But not for long. Suddenly the first Stuart hit the brakes. In front of it was a barricade across the road, and this was not one of those that the GIs mocked at as 'sixty-one minute barricade' – one minute to destroy and sixty minutes to laugh at. This was fully defended. A red blur headed straight for the tank, followed by a stream of black. 'Panzerfaust' someone yelled as the rocket skewered a hole through the Stuart's side. Another of Baum's tanks lurched forward and sent the barricade flying. They rumbled on – straight into a column of twelve Nazi trucks!

The American light tanks' 37mm cannon blasted away. Vehicle after vehicle slewed to a stop, littering the street at crazy angles. Screams started coming from the stricken trucks as the smoke began billowing up. The tanks showed no mercy. It was rarely that their gunners had had such easy targets as these. Without even stopping, they clattered past their victims, all well alight now.

The Task Force hit the River Main again on the eastern bank, where it plunges in a broad 'S' between Aschaffenburg and Würzburg. To the left lay high wooded hills, to the right the road to Gemünden, the first large town that Baum would encounter. He didn't like the situation one bit. Surely the Krauts must be alerted by now and waiting for him. He ordered radio silence and they pushed on. They had reached the outskirts of the town when they were stopped at a railway line. A long train was puffing slowly by, not suspecting that the suddenly stalled column was American. Without orders the lead gunner opened up and the locomotive came to a halt, smoke pouring from its ruptured boiler. But more trains were coming; there seemed to be a never-ending stream of them.

As Captain Baum recalled after the war, 'All along the railroad there were trains. I estimate there must have been about twelve trains, each consisting of twenty cars. It was just getting light and then I realized I had run into something.'

He had. The trains were sitting ducks as the tanks veered to the right along the side of the line. One after another they were shot up until, in half an hour, Baum's troopers had knocked out six of the *Reichsbahn*'s remaining locomotives.

Then they began to move cautiously into Gemünden. At first things seemed to go all right. Businessmen walking to work, briefcases under their arms, stared at the tanks, but took no particular notice of them. They had seen enough tanks over the last years and none of them appeared to notice that these soldiers were wearing a strange kind of helmet. Unfortunately, at just about this time Corporal Frank Malinski, a tank gunner, spotted another train about to leave the station opposite. His 76mm cannon cracked into action and the train came to a halt. Malinski fired again and the train started to burn.

This was the signal for the battle to begin. Unknown to Baum, a whole German division had just arrived at Gemünden and now they set to heartily, eager to annihilate the intruders. Tracer zipped back and forth, but Baum was not prepared to give in. He forced a path through the defenders, ignoring the fire coming from both sides of the cobbled street which led to the vital bridge he needed to take if he was to reach the road to Hammelburg. But he was taking casualties all the time, including some of his officers.

But his luck still held. Somehow an American propaganda outfit had found its way into the middle of the one-sided battle. Under the command of a fluent German speaker Ernst Langendorf, who had been born in Germany, the outfit now broadcast its usual spiel over its vehicle's loudspeaker: 'The war's over. Why fight any longer. Hitler's crazy; he'll soon be dead. We treat German prisoners according to the Geneva Convention. There'll be American cigarettes . . .'

The cigarettes did it! The Germans began to drop their rifles and come out with their hands up, all eager to get their paws on those cigarettes. In the end Langendorf counted 300 of them.

But Baum knew nothing of Langendorf's efforts on his behalf and the German-American returned to his own lines, unaware that he had taken part in a do-or-die battle. When questioned on Task Force Baum, Langendorf shrugged his shoulders and said he'd never heard of the outfit.

From now onwards Task Force Baum vanished into the unknown. That Monday morning Baum sent his first and only message back to 4th Division HQ. It read: 'Send air to attack Gemünden Marshalling Yards'. Thereafter he and his depleted Task Force disappeared from human ken.

IV

THERE'S ONLY ONE THING
WORSE THAN FIGHTING WITH
ALLIES, AND THAT IS
FIGHTING WITHOUT THEM

On the same day that Task Force Baum disappeared in Central Germany, some forty miles behind enemy lines, the Allied Supreme Commander worked out his plans for the remaining months of the war. At Rheims, where he lived in the requisitioned château of one of the great champagne barons of the region, he led a life totally remote from the GIs at the front. He had his mistress, his poker-playing cronies, his 'darkie' orderlies (as he called them) to help him in and out of his silk underwear and a constant stream of visiting 'firemen', ranging from Marlene Dietrich to batches of self-seeking Congressmen, enjoying the military gravy train.

Naturally he paid a high price for these perks. He had high blood pressure and suffered from piles and nervous tension, which he tried to keep at bay with the sixty cigarettes he chain-smoked daily and his only reading matter – Westerns.

Of late he had very nearly reached breaking point – not because of the enemy, but on account of the Allies, in particular, Field Marshal Montgomery. Ever since the previous December during the Battle of the Bulge when Eisenhower had been forced to let Monty take over the command of more American soldiers than were commanded by his own US Army Group Chief, the latter had been a thorn in his side. There had been so much discord between Monty and Bradley and Patton that Bradley had declared he would rather resign than take orders from Montgomery.

Now the time had come to rearrange his strategy so that Montgomery would be given a minor rôle in the battle to come, and the Americans, in particular Bradley and Patton, would be given the kudos of final victory. After all there were three Americans in Europe for every British soldier. And there was a personal consideration too. As Patton had already remarked maliciously to his cronies, Ike was already running for president. Like all successful senior generals in the past, from Washington to Grant, he would be approached by one of the two main US political parties once the war was over to run for the presidency on that party's ticket. It would not look good for a future President if he had given a Britisher the fruits of victory in Europe.

This meant that the main thrust into the Reich towards Berlin in the north, which would come under Montgomery's sphere of influence, would have to be changed. Back on 15 September, 1944, he had written to Montgomery, 'Clearly Berlin is the main prize and . . . there is no doubt in my mind that we should concentrate all our energies and resources on a rapid thrust to Berlin.' Now, six months later, in a signal to General Marshal in Washington, the US Chief-of-Staff, he wrote, 'May I point out that Berlin itself is no longer a particularly important objective. Its usefulness to the German has been largely destroyed and even his government is preparing to move to another area,'

In the place of Berlin, Eisenhower now proposed 'at the earliest possible moment, in conjunction with the Soviets, to divide and destroy the German forces by launching my main attack from the Kassel area straight eastward toward the heart of what remains of the German industrial power.' Thereafter 'I will thrust columns south-eastward in an attempt to join up with the Russians in the Danube valley and prevent the establishment of a Nazi fortress in southern Germany.'

In other words, the three main US Armies, the 7th, 3rd and 1st, would gain the fruits of final victory over the Nazis and be *seen* doing so by the Great American Public back home. But what of Field Marshal Montgomery? The 'Victor of El Alamein' could not be left out of the final battle altogether.

As far back as the Quebec Conference President Roosevelt had come to an agreement with Churchill that, although the British would occupy North-Western Germany, the Americans would be allowed to use Bremen and Bremerhaven in the future British Zone of Occupation, thus freeing the US Army from having to rely upon a line of supply through France. Roosevelt distrusted General de Gaulle, who, he felt, was concerned solely with French interests. In December, 1944, that distrust had deepened during the German attack on Alsace.* Hard-pressed by the Germans, Eisenhower proposed to de Gaulle that the Allied armies should evacuate Strasbourg, the Alsatian capital, to shorten the American line. De Gaulle's reaction was frightening. Through his Chief-of-Staff, Marshal Juin, he informed Eisenhower's equivalent, General Bedell Smith, that the French Army would disobey any such order.

Furthermore, instead of shortening the line, the French 1st Army itself would take over the defence of Strasbourg. Smith's hot temper, fuelled by a grumbling ulcer, flared. 'Is that so?' he rasped. 'It is insubordination, pure and simple. The French First Army will not get a single further round of ammunition or a gallon of petrol.'

Now it was Juin's turn to grow excitable. 'All right,' he snapped, 'in that case General de Gaulle will forbid American forces the use of French railways and communications.'

Bedell Smith knew what that meant. If de Gaulle stopped Allied supplies coming through Cherbourg and Marseilles all hell would be let loose. This was a major crisis and for the time being he backed off, but later he told Eisenhower, 'Juin said things to me last night, which, if he had been an American, I would have socked him on the jaw.'

Later, with Churchill's assistance, a compromise was reached, but Roosevelt didn't trust de Gaulle and saw that the US Army in Germany could not be put in a situation in which it would have to rely on the French for supply and communications. (From what was to happen later it became clear that the dying

* See C. Whiting, *Operation Northwind: the Other Battle of the Bulge* for further details.

61

President had made the right decision.) All supplies for the future US Army of Occupation would have to come through the zone held by the more reliable British. Hence the ports of Bremen, Bremerhaven and Hamburg, indeed the whole area fringing the North Sea, started to loom larger in Eisenhower's calculations.

Now, in his signal to Marshall, he made it clear that Monty would be given a rôle in forthcoming operations after all. Instead of driving for Berlin, he would swing north and seize Lübeck, just east of Hamburg. This would cut off the million and a half German troops in North Germany, Denmark and Norway. At the same time it would prevent the Red Army penetrating further westwards to the mouth of the Baltic. Finally Montgomery would be responsible for securing Bremen/Bremerhaven as the major supply port for US troops in Germany.

When Montgomery heard the news, he regarded it as a severe blow to his pride. Seemingly he had been relegated to the rôle of protecting Bradley's northern flank. In addition with the resources available to him, it seemed to Monty a very tall order. Not only was he to cut off all German troops in the Schleswig-Holstein peninsula before the Red Army could arrive and push on into Denmark, but he also had to take the major fortified position of Bremen, the defences of which he knew little about.

Naturally the British didn't like the new proposals. As Field Marshal Brooke, Chief of the Imperial General Staff, commented when he heard of Ike's change of plan, '[the decision was made] due to national aspirations and to ensure that the US effort will not be lost under British command'. As he wrote in his diary, 'It is a pity . . . straightforward strategy is being affected by the nationalistic outlook of the allies . . . But, as Winston says, "There is only thing worse than fighting with allies and that is fighting without them".'

If Brooke was embittered by the new Eisenhower decision, Montgomery was caught completely off guard by it. In that last week of March, while Patton tried the enemy defences on the far side of the Rhine, Monty was busy ensuring that his troops could break out of their bridgehead on the east side of the river. At the same time he was concerned with a new move, the great dash for the River Elbe to the east. There, with the US 9th Army under command, Montgomery would direct the final drive on Berlin, which would bring the war to a speedy end.

Now things had changed dramatically. Montgomery and his staff were confronted by a situation for which they hadn't bargained. They were expected to change their complete axis of advance, away from the Elbe to the north-west.

Here, as far as they knew, they were expected by Eisenhower not only to tackle two heavily fortified ports but also to deal with the estimated one and a half million troops left in Denmark and Norway. Some of these belonged to second-class formations, but certainly not all those in Norway. Here Hitler had been expecting a British invasion ever since the commando raids of 1941. This, allied to the prospect of a Russian attack into Norway from the region of the Arctic Circle, had meant that there had always been large numbers of first-class troops, including those resting from the fighting in Russia, stationed in that country.

And even before the British could reach Bremen and Hamburg, of which they presently knew little, they would be faced with the river lines of Leine, Aller and Weser. Of these they knew more. As Montgomery was soon to signal the War Office to warn Brooke of the dangers to come: 'The general picture in the BREMEN AREA and on the WESER front is of very determined resistance to keep us away from BREMEN and stop us crossing the WESER and ALLER.'

As yet Montgomery really didn't know what he faced in the north. Due to the fact that Hitler believed, thanks to 'Operation Eclipse', that the Rhine Crossing would be accompanied by an enemy air-sea landing in the North Sea area, the German authorities were making an all-out effort to fight Monty in the north. A second Marine Division had been formed and the 8th German Flak Division, which had defended Bremen from allied air attack throughout the war, had been given a ground rôle. It commanded 100 of the feared 88mm guns, plus about the same number of smaller calibre artillery pieces, many of them 'meat choppers'.* The *Volkssturm* had been called to the colours throughout Northern Germany, their ranks augmented by

* Name given to the German quadruple 20mm quick-firing cannon.

teenagers and workers culled from the great factories in the area. More and more sailors without ships were impressed into 'alarm units' and 'battle groups'. These men, mostly fit twenty-year-olds, might not have received much infantry training, but they made up for it with their determination, even fanaticism.

So, even with what little he knew of the German defences in the north, Montgomery was aware of a tough fight ahead with the three corps of some seventeen divisions available to him. * Naturally he intended to bypass centres of resistance, but still he had to force those three river lines – they couldn't be avoided. Nor could he bypass the outlying penisulas, islands and estuaries that surrounded Bremen/Bremerhaven. He had done that the previous September when his 11th Armoured Division had captured Antwerp by *coup de main*. But his troops had failed to clear the Scheldt estuary leading from Antwerp to the sea, with the result that the port had been closed for supplies for a further two months until he launched a two-and-a-half division attack to clear the estuary.

So, while Montgomery's staff rushed up truckload after truckload of bridging equipment needed to cross the three river lines in front of Bremen and Intelligence desperately sought whatever they could find out on which to base a plan of attack on the port, Montgomery ordered General Brian Horrocks' XXX Corps, the biggest in the British Army, consisting of one armoured division and four infantry, to concentrate on capturing the city. This left the British Second Army, with only three divisions, to advance towards and cross the River Elbe, which had hitherto been its prime objective.

But from news now coming in from the River Main front, where Patton's 3rd Army was doing the most of the fighting in the US Zone of Operations, it was clear that the capture of Bremen was not going to be a walkover.

* For a while that spring the Free Polish Armoured Division, badly needed by Monty, vanished from the line of battle, when the Poles discovered a huge German camp full of sex-starved Polish slave workers.

V

OTHERWISE MY MEN WILL FIRE INTO THE COMPOUND . . . IS THAT UNDERSTOOD?

It was two o'clock on the afternoon of Tuesday, 27 March, 1945, when General von Goeckel, the elderly German general in charge of *Oflag* Hammelburg, was alerted by the sound of tank artillery close to his hilltop camp.

For a year von Goeckel, who had no respect for his American prisoners – 'an ill-disciplined mob'[*] – had had a cushy time since taking over the Hammelburg Camp with its mainly Serb prisoners. Now he realized that he was going to have to earn his pay again. Already his elderly guards were running to take up their positions and he could see the first American light tanks crawling across the ranges two miles away from *Oflag VII*.

Now he was expected to defend Hammelburg with his 300 elderly guards and men of the local *Volkssturm* against US armour, presumably manned by first-class troops, with the possibility that the 'ill-disciplined mob' would run amok once they became aware of what was going on. Already he could see that the half-starved POWs, whose diet most days consisted of 'green hornet soup', a mysterious concoction on the surface of which floated green insects, regarded by them as a good source of protein, were beginning to loot the cookhouses. He realized, as the gunfire grew louder, that severe measures were needed. He was a kindly old man who should have been sent out to grass

[*] Letter to the author.

65

long ago, but now he ordered Colonel Goode, the senior US officer, to keep his men under control. 'Otherwise my men will fire into the compound with their machine guns. Is that understood?'

Not far from the office where the General issued his threat to Goode Baum watched with horror as the battle started to develop around Hammelburg Camp. For an unexpected ally had just reached von Goeckel – a troop of huge German self-propelled guns which packed a far more powerful punch than Baum's Shermans. Already his armour was beginning to take casualties and the attack was beginning to stall. The first Sherman was hit and skidded to a stop. Another came to a halt, a great hole skewered in its side, smoke already beginning to pour from its engine.

The German SP gunners now turned their attention on the soft-skinned vehicles further down the hill. Baum knew he had to do something, and do it quick or his column would be totally wiped out. As he remembered after the war, 'The Krauts' tanks knocked out five of my halftracks and three jeeps, one of them the medic jeep.' One of the stricken halftracks was carrying fuel and ammunition. It went up in flames immediately, with shells bursting into the afternoon sky. With half his column wrecked and burning, Baum ordered a retreat. In reverse, the remaining Shermans started to scuttle back to Hammelburg itself, under the cover of smoke. German artillery Captain Koehl, in charge of the SPs, which held their position, ordered a ceasefire. His crews had had enough. So, it appeared, had the Americans. All the same, Koehl knew they'd be back.

For his part Captain Baum was in something of a quandary. He barely had sufficient vehicles intact to get his survivors back to the other side of the River Main. But he knew that he would have to take some of the POWs back with him. Already, elated by their supposed deliverance, some of the prisoners were breaking through the perimeter fence, ignoring the firing of their elderly guards, and were heading in the general direction of their rescuers.

But the man Baum had really come to rescue was nowhere to be seen. Now he knew for certain that the raid, involving 400 GIs and thirty-odd vehicles, had been planned at the very top, at Patton's 3rd Army HQ, to save one American, and one American only – and so far Lieutenant-Colonel John Waters, Patton's son-in-law and husband of the General's beloved daughter 'Little B', had not approached the embattled rescue party.

Waters' capture in Tunisia in 1943 had come as a great shock to the Patton family, in particular to the General, who regarded Waters as his favourite son-in-law. Over the years Patton had followed Waters' progress through the German POW camps as best he could. When he had heard, in March, 1945, that Waters was only a matter of miles away in Hammelburg's *Oflag VII*, he had decided that he would send a task force to rescue him. That had been the real reason for the dispatch of Task Force Baum.

Now things had gone disastrously wrong both outside the camp and inside. Waters had ventured from his hut in the midst of the firing in the mistaken belief that he could convince the guards to surrender. He didn't get far. Suddenly a German in some sort of camouflaged uniform loomed up out of the smoke of battle. He challenged Waters in German, but Waters did not respond. The German fired from the hip and the slug hit Waters at fifteen yards' range. The German wanted to finish him off, but another guard dissuaded him and arranged to carry him away. He was laid on a makeshift operating table, where a fellow POW, a Serbian surgeon, managed to save his life. As far as the rescue of Colonel Waters was concerned, the raid was already a failure.

There comes a time in battle when even the most experienced soldier makes a mistake. One thinks of Napoleon at Waterloo or Rommel before El Alamein, plagued by dysentery and head-aches. But in most cases the wrong decision is due to a series of minor factors – and exhaustion. It was probably exhaustion, and the non-appearance of Colonel Waters, which made Captain Baum sit on his backside for the next few vital hours when all around him the Germans were preparing to deal him a death blow. In essence Baum wasted too much time at Hammelburg before he decided to move on. But by then it would be too late.

While Baum hesitated, the Germans were hastily scratching together tanks, combat engineers and, more importantly, a battalion of SS infantry to deal with this bold intruder who had succeeded in penetrating sixty miles behind their front line. Now, as Baum's men of the 4th Armored and the prisoners who had managed to escape and join the rescue column, settled down on the high plateau which Baum had selected for his base, Germans were slipping through the darkness like predatory wolves. Armoured troops in the vehicles were already beginning to grind their way up the steep hill and all the time signal flares kept hissing into the sky, bathing the countryside below in their eerie light.

It was about now that Baum wrenched himself from his trance. Suddenly he realized the danger of just waiting there, leaving the initiative to the Krauts, and he ordered his column to move out. But already it was too late. The German infantry, armed with their lethal one-shot bazookas, were waiting for him and his men in the ditches on both sides of the exit road.

'We started back,' Baum recalled after his release from German captivity, 'and hadn't gone fifty yards when we lost a second vehicle to a bazooka. I had to change my direction, so I took a compass bearing and went to the south-west.' Now the battered task force was jolting and bumping its way down a rutted farm track, while, unknown to Baum, three German columns of infantry and tanks were converging on him. But the farmtrack petered out and Baum had to make another decision. 'West,' he concluded in the end and the column, with its wounded ex-PoWs clinging to the tanks, began moving once more. But Baum's worries were increasing by the minute. For the new trail showed evidence of fresh tank tracks. All that Baum could hope for was that they were from tanks of the task force that had been separated from the main body. And in the event it did turn out to be one of his reconnaissance tanks – and it reported some good news. They had found a little road, seemingly unoccupied by the enemy, that ran to Hessdorf, on the Würzburg–Hammelburg highway. It might be the escape route that Baum sought.

For a while things did indeed go well. But as they passed through the next village all hell broke loose. Bursts of fire headed for the American tanks. The Germans couldn't miss. Their first round killed the nearest tank commander. The next swatted the group of ex-PoWs from its deck.

Enemy machine guns on both sides of the narrow street joined it. More former prisoners were hosed from the Shermans' decks. The tanks were sitting ducks and within as many minutes three of them were blazing fiercely.

But, surprisingly enough, the Germans didn't press home their advantage. Their fire died away and Baum had the chance to make a decision. He knew he couldn't force the prepared position which he sensed was further up the village street. He no longer had the strength. As he recounted later, 'I had lost a tank commander and a large group of infantrymen. Knowing I couldn't mess around there, I backed out of the area to assemble the organization on Hill 427, a mile east of [the village of] Hollrich.'

It was a fatal decision. He was heading for the high ground, as soldiers who are at the end of their tether often do. But although he would have the advantage of the heights of Hill 427, he would be also isolated and open to encirclement. It was the same kind of decision which had been the downfall of another dashing cavalry officer six decades earlier – General Custer.

Up on the hill, during a lull in the action, Baum took stock of his situation. PoWs, stimulated by their new-found freedom, bombarded him with suggestions. Finally his patience ran out and he rounded on them, telling them 'to take off' if they wanted to. He was 'goddam sick of them'. Some did, and he never saw them again.

His position, he knew, was lousy. He had started off with 300-odd men and a whole company of armour. Now, as he put it later, 'I could barely scrape together two platoons, about 110 men. I had three medium and three light tanks left, plus one command tank. The halftracks were full of non-serious casualties and the infantry were on the tanks.' This and six former PoWs who had remained with him was the sum total of his force facing elements of two German divisions and an SS battalion.

He knew he had only a few hours of darkness left to effect his escape, but did he have fuel enough to do so? A check showed that he had enough for thirty-five to forty miles. So he had the petrol siphoned off from the halftracks and then had the halftracks set alight, a foolish thing to do in retrospect, as it pinpointed his position to the advancing Germans.

Now he made his decision. He would retreat. Leaving the seriously wounded behind, he gave the order for one last time to mount up. Then the Germans attacked in strength. They hit the Americans from three sides. Suddenly the SS were in among the tanks, running from Sherman to Sherman firing from the hip. Baum abandoned his own vehicle and ran past the fiercely burning Shermans with a handful of his men, trying to break out with those he could save. To no avail. Every time he emerged from the thick firs, which covered the hill like spike-helmeted Prussian guardsmen, he was met by severe fire and forced to turn back. The end was near.

But a battle does not end after the last shot has been fired. Just as when a stone is thrown into a pond and the ripples spread outward, so it is with a battle. For some it means medals and annual parades. For others it is a lifetime thinking and re-thinking that awful moment when it happened. So, in a way, it was with those who survived Task Force Baum. For the Hammelburg PoWs who were recaptured and the new ones from the 4th Armored Division the suffering went on. The few who had escaped the final débâcle were hunted down in the German Spessart Mountains. As for the Army Commander who had dispatched them on that dangerous mission, he lived on in a highly nervous state, knowing that he risked dismissal if it were found what he had done. He was on the defensive, fielding the correspondents' questions as best he could, maintaining that he knew nothing of the 'supposed disappearance of two companies of men from the Fourth. [These were] just malicious rumours' posed by newspapermen out to get him, as they had done in 1943 in Sicily and again a year later in England.

Virtually at once he replaced the two missing companies in the 10th Armored Infantry and the 37th Tank Battalions. When the German radio reported a US armoured unit exterminated far behind their lines, Patton ordered the 3rd Army spokesman to give out a vague press release on a '4th Armored Divisional raiding expedition', sent out 'south-east towards Nuremberg'. There was no mention of Hammelburg and no convincing explanation as to the purpose of this 'raiding expedition'.

A few survivors reached the lines of US General Eddy's corps.

Eddy, who would be sent home on account of 'high blood pressure', couldn't stop the rumours circulating. They reached as high as the Army Group Commander, Bradley, who dismissed the Baum attack as 'a wild-goose chase'. As for the escapees and the few ex-Hammelburg PoWs who came with them, they were flown at once to Camp Lucky Strike in France, where they jumped the lines of the several thousand other ex-PoWs waiting to be repatriated and were shipped home to the States immediately. There, Patton hoped, they would be safe from grilling by those inquisitive war correspondents out to get him. A week later Patton's favourite division was pulled out of the firing line. Its wartime career was over and the commander of the US 3rd Army felt he had covered up his tracks pretty effectively. Let the correspondents talk, but all they had to go on were wild guesses and rumours. Those who really knew what had happened had been removed from the scene. They had been shipped out and, in the case of Colonel Waters and Captain Baum, who had been wounded in the final battle, had been repatriated and were on their way to hospitals in the States.

But Patton was wrong, at least as far as the Top Brass was concerned. From Eisenhower down to General Hoge, commanding the 4th Armored, they knew that Patton had authorized a raid deep behind the German lines for personal reasons and had lost some 400 men, plus perhaps another 100 PoWs, at Hammelburg.[*] It was something that they would use to fire Patton after the war when he was no longer needed in battle. But at the beginning of April none of them seemed to see the significance of the German resistance to what was really no more than a minor US raid.

Naturally it was clear to the US Top Brass that, due to the American superiority in air and armour, they could move at will. The 'rat race' was a true description of the fluid situation beyond the Rhine. However, what they did not seem able to comprehend was that, once their forces hit a fortified position such as

---

[*] Patton died in December, 1945, but his loyal supporters managed to cover up for him for over a quarter of a century. Even then the whole truth about Task Force Baum was not revealed. See the author's *48 Hours to Hammelburg* for his assessment of the raid.

Hammelburg Camp, the Germans would fight all out. In essence any German town, even at this late stage of the war, could become another Aachen. Soldiers and civilians would all join in to fight to the very last in street battles where US armour and air support were of little or no value.

Now, as the US Armies, mainly the 3rd and 7th, began to cross the River Main in force, heading for the Alpine Redoubt, they would be faced by a string of fortified German cities. Running from west to east they included Stuttgart, Aschaffenburg, Nuremberg, Munich, and so on, all vital to the Reich's economy. They could all have been left to wither on the vine, but Bradley and his subordinate commanders seemed still to be sticking to the old US Army doctrine which stated that ground for which men of the US Army had shed their blood *could not* and *would not* be abandoned. Once Americans had given their lives for a piece of real estate, it had to be held as a matter of prestige.

Thus, while Montgomery in the north was already planning a five-division assault on Bremen, which *had* to be taken, on Eisenhower's orders, the attack and capture of those other fortified cities to the south was being left to the decisions and half-hearted planning of local commanders, down to divisional level. It was a recipe for high losses which could have been avoided and an unnecessary prolonging of the war in Europe.

3

MARCH – APRIL, 1945

I

SEE FORTY-FIVE AND SURVIVE

On 27 March, 1945, the 'Thunderbirds'* of the veteran 45th Division, belonging to the 7th Army, began their attack on Aschaffenburg. The city was one of the great treasure-houses of medieval art and architecture, and home to some 60,000-odd civilians. But it was also a centre of modern German industry, in particular the place where many of Germany's latest jet fighter-planes were produced. As the 'Thunderbird' men would learn in due course, it was also a German fortress.

The division had first gone into action in Sicily in July, 1943, then in Italy and right through France the following year, and on into Germany to the Rhine which they had just crossed. The men were confident and experienced. But by now the Division's confident motto of 'Live to '44 and see the end of the war' had become a more sober 'See '45 and survive'. Still, they didn't think the fortress of Aschaffenburg would put up much of a fight. But they were in for a surprise.

So far in their rapid fifty-seven-kilometre advance from the Rhine eastwards the Division had passed through nothing but deserted villages inhabited by tame civilians; 'dead-faced women and old men who glared with unfathomable bitterness or simply looked blank while the great serpentine stream of American soldiers and vehicles passed'. But the passive attitude of these civilians was soon to end.

On 28 March the first patrols had returned to report that there were a lot of German bunkers defending the city's perimeter, but that the defenders had done little to hinder the progress of

* After the 45th's divisional patch, an Indian Thunderbird totem.

the squads probing the outskirts. If Aschaffenburg was a fortress, as the Germans had proclaimed, it had not shown itself to be much of one.

The 45th Division's 157th Regiment kicked off the attack in line abreast the following morning. This regiment crossed the Main in a four-battalion assault. At first the GIs met little opposition. But once they started to plod warily up the steep bank on the other side of the river all hell was let loose. The grim old song of death began once more. Tracer scythed the slope. Mortars tore the foliage apart and trees snapped like matchwood. At that range the well-dug-in Germans, who had been watching the Americans for hours, now couldn't miss. GIs went down on all sides.

The sister regiment of the 157th had an easier approach at first. The 179th Motorized Infantry drove to the River Main and began crossing in the 157th's zone of operation. They heard the firing in the distance, but the battlefield was shrouded in smoke and they paid little attention. They had almost breasted the bank when the Germans attacked, running at the surprised GIs, yelling and screaming. With them came civilians, not the tame submissive old men and boys they had encountered all the previous week, but men as fanatical as the soldiers of the 15th Grenadier Replacement Depot who were defending the heights.

The Americans began to go to ground, digging foxholes with more speed and determination than they had done for a long time. As they did so the German 105mm multiple mortars further back opened up with a deafening roar. In groups of three, the shells shrieked across the sky, trailing thick black smoke behind them, and when the shells struck home the very ground seemed to shiver. Slowly but surely the initial attack of the Thunderbird Division began to peter out.

Ascheffenburg's defences were commanded by one of those fanatical last-ditch German units which the advancing Allied troops were now beginning to encounter everywhere. Put in charge of a *Festung*, they signed the oath to defend it to the last man and the last bullet without hesitation. Major von Lambert, the fortress commander at Aschaffenburg, was one such. He would fight to the very end, even if it meant the destruction of the beautiful medieval city. Despite his aristocratic name, he was a ruthless bully of the worst kind; to him human life meant nothing. In the course of the next days, not only would he sacrifice his uniformed soldiers, stringing up or shooting those who would not fight, but he made boys and women fight to the very last under pain of death. The fight for Aschaffenburg would take the Americans six days. For most of the defenders, men of the 15th Grenadiers and the German 36th Infantry Division, seemed just as fanatically inclined as their commander. As the historian of the 45th Division wrote at the end of the war: '[They were] boys of sixteen and seventeen, thoroughly indoctrinated with the theory that it was glorious to seek death for the Fatherland'. He didn't add that the veterans of the Division were happy to help them on their way to 'glory', killing the kids in their foxholes when they seemed disinclined to accept the first offer by the Americans to surrender.

The first day of the 45th's attack had been bad; the second was even worse. As dawn broke, the Germans attacked, urged on by their NCOs, who, armed with sub-machine guns, brought up the rear to ensure that there was no wavering among the attackers. For a while, it was touch and go, but finally the Germans were beaten off and the GIs started to push into the suburbs of the city, which would be completely ruined before Ascheffenburg was finally taken.

Now street fighting began, for artillery and tanks were of little use in the narrow streets. As one of the Thunderbirds recalled, 'House-cleaning by force always meant sudden death for someone. It means kicking in a door and lobbing in a grenade and then charging in to see who's still alive, who wants to surrender and who wants to die!'

Major von Lambert now organized old men, women and girls to fill out the thinning ranks of the defenders. They hurled grenades from the rooftops of the buildings, but the GIs shot them down just as they would have done any enemy soldier in uniform.

General Frederick, the youthful commander of the 45th Division, asked for air support to blast the stubborn defenders from the smoking ruins. The commander of the P-47 fighter-bomber squadron detailed to fly the mission was dubious, but he said he'd have a go. Due to the close proximity of the

American troops to the Germans, he was only prepared to use fifty-calibre machine-gun ammunition, not bombs, which would have been too dangerous for the GIs.

This didn't work, so the next time the airmen picked out specific targets the whereabouts of which American Intelligence had gained from German prisoners. One such was Aschaffenburg's Gestapo HQ, which the 45th believed was being used to direct the city's defences. The P-47s zoomed in, braving what appeared to be a solid wall of 20mm flak, and pinpointed their target with light bombs and rockets.

The bombs dropped straight on to their target and began to explode on the Gestapo HQ. For the first time in Europe napalm, which hitherto had been reserved for the battle against inferior Orientals in the Pacific, was being employed against white people. The napalm bombing of the Aschaffenburg Gestapo HQ was indicative of just how seriously the American High Command regarded the situation. For Eisenhower had given specific permission for the attack, despite the fact that he knew there would be an outcry back home once they heard of it. Napalm was reserved for 'slopeheads' and 'gooks'.

At the same time as the napalm attack the frustrated US Top Brass in SHAEF HQ were actively considering whether civilians bearing arms in Aschaffenburg would be shot there and then on the spot where they were taken prisoner. As far as is known no order was given on this score, but in the event both civilian and military prisoners *were* shot. Men, women and children were mercilessly eliminated by the GIs of the 45th Infantry Division, especially if they were snipers. The GIs *hated* the enemy snipers, whatever their age, sex or status.

Still the Germans continued their stubborn defence. Prisoners told their captors that they had no choice but to fight to the bitter end. According to the PoWs' statements, when individual groups decided they could or would not fight any longer, heavily armed SS or police would descend upon them and their leaders would be strung up from the nearest lamppost and the SS officers would place a cardboard placard on the dead man's chest, bearing such legends as: 'Here Died a Defeatist' or 'Death to All Traitors'. One captured Hungarian in the service of the *Wehrmacht* said that when he and some of his comrades had tried to bolt from the death trap, most of them had been shot in the back by the SS.

On the third day, General Frederick decided that he was wasting too much time and too many valuable lives on Aschaffenburg, so he ordered two of his three regiments to bypass the place and continue their advance. But, true to that pernicious US Army doctrine that ground bought with American blood should never be relinquished, he left his 157th Regiment to maintain what had now become a traditional siege. The battle for Aschaffenburg was developing into a second Aachen!

On Easter Sunday, 1945, a GI who had been captured earlier on was sent back to the American lines, accompanied by a German *Hauptmann*. The captain had brought with him a message from Major von Lambert saying that he would negotiate a surrender if the Americans would send an emissary to his headquarters, but Colonel O'Brien, the commander of the 157th, refused to bargain. His temper was up and he told the German to tell his superior that, if Lambert did not immediately have white flags of surrender waved over his HQ, the aerial bombardment would be intensified. This time they'd drench the place in napalm and no one would escape.

The threat worked. Although the Americans had guessed wrongly, that von Lambert's HQ was in the Gestapo headquarters, white flags started to flutter over his real command post – the Renaissance castle. Half an hour later the battered survivors, including von Lambert, who had taken his own life as he had sworn to do, came filing out, hands raised, into the dusty sunshine of an April afternoon. The six-day siege was over and 1,000 German prisoners went into the American cages. What happened to von Lambert is not recorded. He disappeared from the scene to become yet another grim footnote to the history of the Second World War.

II

THEY WASN'T NUTHIN' BUT KIDS

The news that Aschaffenburg had been so strongly defended when everyone thought that the Germans were finished came as a shock to the American Top Brass. Bradley, who was behind Eisenhower's decision to change the whole thrust of the Allied attack towards the supposed Alpine Redoubt, was particularly surprised, but in public he dismissed it as a one-off affair. The Germans had fought so well and for so long because they had the advantage of long-prepared defences. As far back as 1935, 'a belt of River Main defenses' had been created 'in anticipation of some French retaliation when Hitler remilitarized the Rhineland.'

Others were not so sanguine, particularly back in the States, and predicted that there would be more Aschaffenburgs. Stimson, the US Secretary of State for Defense, told the press, 'There is a lesson with respect to this in Aschaffenburg. These Nazi fanatics used the visible threats of two hangings to compel German soldiers and civilians to fight.' He went on to say that he now intended to warn the enemy that 'their only choice is immediate surrender or the destruction of the Reich, city by city.'

Still Bradley persisted in his stubborn plan of attacking one fortified city after another, although Allen Dulles, the head of the OSS in Switzerland, was already negotiating with the Germans, including Himmler's personal representative, SS General Wolff, for the surrender of all German troops in Italy, which would have meant the end of the Redoubt, even if it had existed. Yet Bradley, who knew of these talks, was telling visiting US congressmen as late as 24 April, 'We may be fighting one month from now, and it may even be a year.'

Heilbronn, held by a mixed bag of Hitler Youth and SS, was attacked, although it could have been avoided. Under determined leadership, these 'soldiers', some as young as fourteen and others as old as sixty, held back a 16,000-strong US Division, the 100th Infantry. Not only did they defend Heilbronn, but they counter-attacked and came within a nick of throwing the 'Centurymen' back across the River Neckar. With the hurriedly called up assistance from the US 10th Armored Division, the Americans managed to hang on, but the subsequent assault took another three days of bitter house-to-house combat. It was almost as if the US Army in Southern Germany was going out of its way to look for trouble.

Whatever the Top Brass's motives were, young men were still dying fighting the 'beaten' Germans. And the kids of the Hitler Youth were the worst. One company commander, Lieutenant Slade of the 100th Division's 397th Infantry, remembers how, after a terrific mortar barrage on their positions, the group of Hitler Youth holding up his attack finally panicked and broke. Screaming *'Kamerad'*, they flung up their arms and bolted for the American lines. Their officers showed no mercy and blasted the backs of the running youths. Six of them fell dead. Thirty-six made it. 'They wasn't nuthin' but kids,' Slade commented later. 'Before the mortars hit them they fought like demons, but now they were only a disorganized mass of fourteen to seventeen year olds.'

But again and again the Top Brass sent their young men to attack fortified German positions. General Morris's 10th Armored Division, which had helped to save the day at Heilbronn, was sent to take Crailsheim, and did so without too much difficulty. Then the tankers were attacked by two groups of SS troopers and the balloon went up. Belonging to the best German division still fighting in Bavaria, the 17th SS Panzer Grenadier Division, 500 troopers, plus a further 700, attacked the town on both flanks. The Americans were taken by surprise. They hadn't expected a counter-attack, especially one pressed home with such determination. Supported by twenty-five of the new, twin-engined Messerschmitt fighter-bombers, which zoomed in on the American positions at 600mph, the SS succeeded, on the second day of their surprise attack, in surrounding the town and cutting off all 10th Armored's supply routes save one, and this one was under constant attack from ground and air. As Richard Johnston, correspondent of the *New York Times*, was told by General Morris, when he said he was going up that road to interview the trapped troopers, 'Start like a bat out of hell and keep going faster!'

But he didn't make it. The German artillery fire was too intense. That day no supplies reached the trapped Americans, so a force of fifty C-47 carrier planes was assembled for a re-supply operation and to bring out the wounded. But just before the planes were due to land in the fields near the single road they were jumped by three Messerschmitts going all out. But by now the men of the 10th Armored Division were prepared. Light anti-aircraft guns lined the road and they started pumping tracer shells at the attackers, while the deck machine guns of the 10th's Shermans joined in. But the Messerschmitts pressed home their attack through what appeared to be a solid wall of sudden death. Then one of them lost control and slammed into the ground. The rest fled the way they had come.

Soon thereafter the C-47s started to land, while American fighters circled watchfully above them. They landed without loss on a strip only one thousand yards from the German position, and only just in time. As they brought in desperately needed ammunition and gasoline, 600 men of the Austrian Second Mountain Division struck from the south-west and within a few hours had managed to get inside Crailsheim.

Once established, the Austrian mountaineers, who had been fighting the Americans ever since the 7th Army had landed in the south of France the previous summer, called up their reserves, whereupon 600 enemy came charging out of the darkness, supported by heavy self-propelled guns.

Major T. Hankins, who commanded the infantry holding Crailsheim, told the handful of correspondents who had now managed to get through to the beleaguered town, 'We fought 'em off twice and we can fight 'em off again.'

Brave talk. Privately, however, he prayed that the US 63rd Division, which was some fifteen miles away from Crailsheim, would hurry up and relieve them. He knew that the 10th Armored couldn't hold out much longer. Back home in the States the newspapers were calling the besieged Bavarian town 'Bastogne Number Two'.

All that day Crailsheim was attacked from the air. German jets streaked in, leaving the AA gunners helpless to tackle them. They bombed and straffed with impunity. On the ground the SS pelted the Americans with a constant mortar barrage.

That day a Lieutenant Max Schoenberg, who had been bombed out of his command post twice in the last three days, told US correspondent A. Goldberg of Associated Press, 'We're sweating this out now,' and his commander butted in to add, 'If they don't throw any more at us than they have done over the last two nights, I think we have enough to hold them. They have been attacking in at least six-company strength and they are tough SS babies of all ages, but mostly twenty to twenty-five.'

But that wasn't to be. The tanks simply couldn't beat the SS veterans and in the end the US 7th Army decided that the defence of Crailsheim was not worth the effort. The one supply road was being constantly mined and ambushed, taking a heavy toll of truck and jeep drivers trying to break through. The verges were littered with wrecked US vehicles and the bloody, silent bundles which had once been young men.

On the night of 11 April, 1945, while the SS watched with incredulity, the last Shermans of Major Hankins' force started slinking out of the town. The Germans had recaptured Crailsheim!*

Four days later Eisenhower announced his strategy for dealing with what was left of the Third Reich. The US Seventh Army would drive south and south-east into Austria. After the battles for Aschaffenburg, Heilbronn and Crailsheim, he thought this might well be a tall order for America's most neglected army, short of both infantry and armour. That same army which had been the US Army's stepchild ever since Patton had created it in 1943 was now showered with Eisenhower's largesse.

---

* Crailsheim was finally taken by the D-Day veterans of the 4th Infantry Division, but not until a Lieutenant Jones and two other men had been treacherously shot in the back while under a white flag. The Division's artillery then blasted the place apart.

The Supreme Commander offered General Patch, the Army Commander, all of SHAEF's reserve divisions, plus the first Allied Air Army, which contained British airborne troops, and the newly arrived 13th US Airborne Division. For the first time since its creation, Patch's army was being given maximum resources, and General Patch knew why. *He* was to tackle the Alpine Redoubt. But first he was committed to capturing Nazi Germany's holiest city, *die Stadt der Bewegung.**

* The City of the Movement (ie the Nazi Movement).

III

THE ROCK OF THE MARNE

Those who had followed the events in Continental Europe in the years before the Second World War had been impressed, perhaps even frightened, by the pictures of the 'New Germany' which had appeared on their newsreels every September. First had come pictures of the medieval spires of the southern Germany city. Then followed shots of hazy, dawn streets slowly coming to life. Then the half-timbered *Gassen* had begun to fill up with smiling peasants, dressed in outlandish rural costumes. They would come – drift would be a better word – out of their cobbled backyards, smoking curved pipes with barefoot children savouring the last of their breakfast. And always in the background there would be a few muted chords of Wagner to indicate that there was some kind of inherent greatness in these homely scenes.

The knowledgeable cinemagoer knew he wouldn't have to wait long for the menacing stamp of hundreds of steel-shod boots on the freshly washed cobbles, the rattle of kettledrums, the shrill of the flutes and then the military band would break into its full bombastic blare. *They* were coming.

'They' were rank after rank of brown-clad stormtroopers. Each 'Hitler-soldier', as the Führer called them, was weighed down with his full pack, water bottle and bread bag. They would stamp, wooden-faced and proud, behind the blood-red flag bearing the legend *'Deutschland erwache'* (Germany awake).

The marchers marked the start of the annual conference of the National Socialist Party, orchestrated by no less a person than the Minister of Propaganda and Public Englightenment, Dr Josef Goebbels. He brought Germans from all over the Third

Reich to pay homage to their leader, Adolf Hitler, who told them proudly and confidently that 'they were the future'.

As the days passed, there would be spectacle after spectacle. Hitler Youth, SA and SS, the Farmers' Union, the Volunteer Work Service, ever more organizations created by the Hitler Government. They would create the 'New Order', which would rid the country of its decadence and replace it with the heady idealism of unspoiled German youth.

And in the end the Führer would sum it all up. Like a conquering hero, he would stride down the central aisle of the flag-bedecked Luitpold Hall, followed by his 'paladins', as he called his brown-clad henchmen, while the brass band blared and thumped out his favourite Badenweiler Inspection March and thirty thousand Party faithful raised their right arms in the 'German Greeting' and bellowed '*Heil Hitler*' over and over again.

By 1939 the old Bavarian city, the second biggest in the state after the capital, Munich, had become something of a legend in Germany, and for those neo-fascists in Europe, and in the United States too, a kind of holy shrine. Nuremberg, the city in question, once famous for its medieval treasures and legendary names such as Dürer, Hans Sachs and the master wood-carver Veit Stoss, had become the infamous *Stadt der Bewegung*.

That knowledge worried General Sandy Patch on two counts. The Army Commander was about at the end of his tether due to the recent death of his son in action and the effect it had had on his wife,* and he was concerned that the diehard Nazis of the well-fortified city's garrison would fight to the bitter end. After all Nuremberg was no ordinary city. Rather, it was a shrine to National Socialism, a holy place dedicated to the Führer. Would the defenders outdo those of Aschaffenburg, Heilbronn and Crailsheim and turn Nuremberg into a bloodbath for themselves and for his own men?

There was one other consideration which his Intelligence team put in front of the dejected Army Commander. In a matter of days a momentous event, for the Nazis at least, would take

---

* Patch died not long after he returned to the States after the war, some said of a broken heart.

1. General Patton fulfils his promise to pee in the Rhine.

2. General Horrocks with his tank driver, Sergeant Stiff.

3. One of Captain De Grineau's drawings of the so-called 'Massacre at Rethem' (p.121-2).

4. The stadium at Nuremberg, the "*Stadt der Bewegung*" (p.86).

5. "Nuremberg had been captured by the Americans" (p.96).

6. "Crocodile' tanks joined in the fight... squirting their deadly flames" (p.156).

7. US troops turn an 88mm cannon against its former owners south of Bremen (see also p.144).

8. Men of the Irish Guards on a recent Battlefield Tour are shown the spot where Eddie Charlton won the VC (see p.169).

9. Brigadier Michael O'Cock meets *Leutnant* Von Bülow for the first time (sep.170).

10. Lübeck falls to the British, 1 May, 1945.

11. The Berghof after its capture in May, 1945 (see p.198).

12. The 51st Highland Division enters Bremerhaven.

13. German *Prominenz* march through the ruins of Bremen to surrender.

14. Major Pope, of the 4th
Wiltshires, who led the raid
on Becker's bunker (see
p.195).

15. Men of the Somerset Light
Infantry and the 4th
Wiltshires outside Becker's
bunker (p.195).

16. General Montgomery with released British prisoners of war at Fallingbostel.

17. Trenches still visible today on the roadside south of Bremen.

place. On 20 April it would be the Führer's 56th birthday, his twelfth since coming to power. Intelligence knew how important his birthday had always been for the Germans. Time and again during the war his soldiers had tried to capture some fortress or take a defended position as a birthday present for Hitler on 20 April. What if the Americans put the boot on the other foot? What a blow it would be for Hitler and his fanatical followers if the city which symbolized their whole creed fell to Americans on that very day! Capture Nuremberg on 20 April, 1945, and what remained of Nazi Germany might well collapse like a house of cards.

After years of intensive bombing by the RAF at night and the US 8th Air Force by day Nuremberg was by now surrounded by a formidable ring of 88mm cannon, which could be used in both a ground and air rôle. Now, as the Americans advanced on the already ruined city – ideal for the kind of infantry battle which would soon develop – these cannon became the backbone of Nuremberg's artillery defence. Nor was that all. With their artillery in place, the Germans now prepared to defend the city with elements of two crack divisions, the 2nd Mountain and the 17th Panzer Grenadier, plus a new *ad hoc* formation, the *Gruppe Grafenwoehr*, two battalions strong and made up of young NCOs and the like who had been instructors and demonstrators at the local Grafenwoehr Training Ground. As such the *Gruppe* was even more formidable than the veteran SS grenadiers.

It was a sizeable force, even for Patch's two veteran 3rd and 45th Divisions, along with the 42nd (Rainbow) Division which would also take part in the assault. But it was made more formidable by the man who was to become the inspiration of the city's defence, *Gauleiter* Karl Holz, a sulky-faced opinionated veteran of the First World War, who was to remain a devoted follower of the Führer to the very last. If anyone was going to stop the Americans it would be Holz.

But on 16 April when the attack started, General Frederick, commanding the 45th Division, and General 'Iron Mike' O'Daniel, commanding the 3rd Division, were not particularly worried by the opposition. Both led reliable outfits. Indeed the Third Infantry Division, 'the Rock of the Marne', as it was called from its exploits in the First World War, was perhaps the most famous infantry unit in the US Army. At a cost of 30,000 casualties, it had won more Congressional Medals for bravery in action than any other American outfit. And both Generals were well aware of the significance of the city to the Nazis and knew that the kudos of capturing it would be rated high in the headlines back home. Besides, O'Daniel had a score to settle. Like Patch, he too had lost a son in action, fighting the Germans in Holland. He wanted his revenge. So, without too much thought, they set the divisions in motion. Before the Führer's birthday they wanted the City of the Movement captured. It was going to be a present, not to the Führer, but to the American people.

On 17 April the three divisions involved in the assault were roughly in position. In a coordinated assault, the 45th Division was to hit Nuremberg from the east, while the Third were to come in from the north. The 42nd Division was to attack the Citadel from the west, driving through what was really a city divided in two – an outer or *Neustadt* (new city) and the inner, walled *Altstadt* (old town).

At first the main opposition came from the sky. The German fighters came in time and again and the gunners of the 3rd's 441st Anti-Aircraft Battalion maintained that they had fired off more shells that day than on any day since they had landed in France the previous summer.

On its flank the 45th Division was subjected to similar massive airstrikes, but the men pressed on, their only encounter of note being with Mrs Fritz Kuhn and her daughter, Waldtraut. The wife of the former leader of the *Bund*, the American Nazi Party, funded from Berlin prior to America's entry into the war, was living comfortably with her ugly daughter in a villa paid for out of local Party funds. The wife of the 'American Führer' was soon behind bars.

The Third was now finding the going difficult. Although most of the tanks and self-propelled guns of *Gruppe Grafenwoehr* were being dealt with by the armour of the US 14th Armored Division north-east of Nuremberg, some of the German mobile cannon, armed with massive 105mm guns, had managed to break through the armoured screen and the Germans began making life hell for the thin-skinned American Shermans and White halftracks. Indeed the Germans were bold enough to counter-attack that Tuesday in order to prevent the Americans throwing a ring of steel round Nuremberg.

But one lone American wasn't going to allow that, for on that day Private Joseph Merrell started a one-man war with the enemy, which would earn him, posthumously, his country's highest honour, the Congressional Medal.

As his company went to ground, pinned down by heavy fire from an SS unit, Merrell charged forward on his own initiative. Zigzagging through a wall of fire, he shot down four Germans at point blank range in as many seconds. Even then he didn't stop, but continued his lone charge until he was spun round as a sniper's bullet slammed into his M-I rifle. He threw it to the ground and ran on, now armed only with three grenades. He closed with a German machine gun which was holding his company at bay, flung two of his grenades at it and dived into the nearest shell hole, prepared, as the Official Citation put it, 'to fight with his bare hands if necessary'.

The grenades exploded, but not all the SS gunners were dead and the survivors were now manning a second machine gun. Merrell grabbed a German pistol from somewhere and prepared to tackle the next machine gun. But he hadn't gone far when a vicious burst from the gun hit him. But he somehow found the strength to throw his final grenade and with it he wiped out the second machine gun. But then he took a burst from an SS man wielding a burp gun at close range and he was dead even before he hit the ground.

Young Joseph Merrell, a youth barely into his twenties, was the first of three brave men of the 3rd Infantry Division to win the Medal of Honor during the assault on Nuremberg that April, ample testimony to the courage of the attackers.

IV

GAULEITER, THE DEFENCE OF NUREMBERG IS CRAZY

Once, as we noted, Nuremberg had been the centre of German culture. Here Hans Sachs, the little cobbler, and his *Meister-sänger*, had flourished. But now twelve years of Nazi domination had taken their toll. 'The land of poets and thinkers' (*Dichter und Denker*), as it had been called in the 19th century, had become that of 'the judges and hangmen' (*Richter und Henker*).

Its *Gauleiter*, Karl Holz, typified this brutal new Germany. As the Americans got closer to his city's ruined centre, he was here, there and everywhere, encouraging, cajoling and threatening the defenders. When the 60-year-old head of the local *Volks-sturm* disbanded his command, sending them home before shooting himself, Holz ordered them to re-form immediately.

It was the same when General Dr Martin told him to his face, '*Gauleiter*, the defence of Nuremberg is crazy. It can't be held.' Holz shouted at the police chief, 'General, I shall have you indicted before a flying court [a court of three officers who passed judgement and sentence on the spot without any form of legal defence] for not carrying out the Führer's orders. I'm reporting this to Himmler immediately.' We don't know whether Holz did. We do know, however, that he would personally shoot the *Oberbürgermeister* Dr Leibel when the latter refused to carry on with the senseless defence of the city.

Three days after the start of the American assault Holz gave out the codeword 'PUMA'. This signified that Nuremberg should be turned into a wasteland as part of Hitler's new scorched earth policy. Under its terms it was envisaged that the city workers would systematically destroy all electricity and gas works, the water supply, the factories, the various inner city bridges, and so on. Fortunately for Nuremberg's surviving citizens, huddled fearfully in the cellars of their ruined houses, most of the city's workers had fled and the order couldn't be carried out.

Still the fanatical Holz kept up his resistance, personally threatening anyone he thought was a coward or a defeatist with his pistol.

Two days before the city finally fell, he cabled Hitler that 'The soldiers are fighting bravely and the population is proud and steadfast. I will stay in this most German city to fight and die. The National Socialist creed will triumph. We greet you, *mein Führer*, the National Socialists of *Gau** Franconia in German loyalty. Karl Holz'.

Then, after he had sent off this piece of high-flown bombast, Holz personally led a raiding party in the area of the main station, to which the Americans had now advanced, returning to tell his cronies proudly, '*Everyone* stays in Nuremberg and will die if necessary.'

It was a sentiment that the Commander of the 3rd Division subscribed to most heartily. He was only too willing to oblige. He'd ensure that anyone still wanting to fight *would* die.

O'Daniel pushed his men hard. Now they had breached the medieval wall that enclosed the city. Relentless house-to-house fighting had reached the stage of no quarter given or expected. In an attempt to get the battle over with more swiftly, O'Daniel sent in tanks. But they proved no match for the Germans lurking on the roofs, who, armed with the *panzerfaust*, could easily knock out the lightly armoured Shermans. In the end it became standard operating procedure for tankers to stand off from any building suspected of containing snipers and blast it apart with their 75mm cannon before the infantry were sent in.

But the heart was going out of the defenders. In one day alone the men of the 45th Division captured ninety 88mm anti-aircraft guns intact, took just short of a thousand prisoners and a huge underground cache of frozen meat and other stores. The GIs'

* A region created by the Nazis and ruled by a *Gauleiter*.

eyes nearly popped out of their heads when they saw the 'goodies', after days, perhaps weeks, of canned rations.

But it wasn't quite over yet. As the History of the 45th records: 'Soldiers told of fighting against children in Nuremberg, boys of 14 years old, who sniped at the Americans or hurled hand grenades.'

On 19 April the 45th launched a three-battalion attack, supported by whatever elements of the weary 3rd O'Daniel could make available. The Germans resisted, as one US correspondent put it, 'like tigers'. The local civilians joined in and Holz even called up the fire brigade.

The defenders went to any lengths to stop the Americans: they booby-trapped their own dead so that when the American aid men picked them up in one last act of mercy they too died violently. The Americans brought up the largest calibre cannon they had available – the 12-M assault gun. Over open sights, the great gun started to batter the enemy positions and those Germans who survived the bombardment and surrendered had mostly gone mad. Slowly but surely the Americans began to force the defenders back. At last it seemed as if they were winning the Battle of Nuremberg. The Top Brass apparently thought so, as they now planned a great ceremony among the ruins to celebrate the city's fall.

Nineteen days before, the only surviving member of his company in the 3rd's 15th Infantry Regiment had written home to his native Texas in his illiterate scrawl: 'Hello everyone, just a few lines to say hello and let you know i am still OK. Heres hoping you are well. Did i tell you that I have been awarded the DSC and a Bronz Star and i already have the Purple Heart and two oak leaf clusters and now in back in Regt Hdqrs waiting for them to give me the CMH so i can come home. Am also to receive the Legion of Merit pretty soon, since that is all the medals they have to offer I'll take it easy for a while, ha ha ha.'

Thus Audie Murphy, the future cowboy star for Paramount and America's most decorated soldier. Soon he would receive his country's highest award, the Medal of Honor. In years to come the 20-year-old infantryman, who was finally forced to become a 'shavetail lieutenant', would pay for that honour. Reputed to have killed at least two hundred Germans, he was to suffer for years from nervous tension.* Now, however, he was looking forward to the presentation of the Medal of Honor to himself and others in the Division.

For the 3rd and 45th were determined to celebrate the capture of Nuremberg, which could only be a matter of hours away now. Already the city's central *Adolf Hitler Platz* had been renamed, rather stupidly, *Eisener Michael Platz* – Iron Mike Square – in honour of the Divisional Commander. Murphy was pleased enough by the award but he didn't care for the bullshit and toadying to the Top Brass which went with it, especially as he felt that the Generals concerned were counting their chickens before they were hatched. Nuremberg was not yet captured.

Murphy was right. On the same day that the GIs of the engineer companies started to prepare the renamed *Adolf Hitler Platz* for what was to come a company of the 'Marnemen' was counter-attacked on both flanks. The Germans were mechanics, ground crews and the like, transferred the day before from *Luftwaffe* fields nearby to the infantry. What they lacked in training and tactics they made up for in dash and daring. While Murphy waited at HQ for the bullshit to begin, the *Luftwaffe* men forced the 'Marnemen' to go to ground. Within the hour they were trapped among the heaps of rubble. Another company of the Third Infantry were whistled up to help their trapped comrades out of the mess in which they found themselves. Less than a mile away the engineers and electricians hammered and sawed away, happily preparing 'Iron Mike Square' for the ceremonies to come, unaware that their comrades might not survive to watch the bullshit to come.

'It was total confusion,' Corporal Cooper of the trapped company recalled years later. 'The Krauts had small mortars shelling the shit out of us all the while. Every time one of us moved, the enemy snipers went to work. Guys stumbled back everywhere, shot through the skull. Naturally the snipers and their bazaookamen were looking for officers and senior

---

* Murphy couldn't sleep. When he went to bed, he always took a .45 pistol with him. In a way, it was a blessing when he died in an air crash at the age of 46.

noncoms. Some of them started pulling off their stripes and insignia. That showed just how bad it was.

'About halfway through the action, till we were relieved, some joker said, "D'ya know Iron Mike's giving away medals this afternoon only a mile from here?" Nobody believed the guy and another guy said, "Medals – *here*? Go and tell that to the Marines." But he was right, not that we ever saw it.'

Karl Holz now threw in his last reserves, a company of middle-aged cops. Most of them had fought as young men in the trenches in the last war and they had no desire to die at the end of this one. Neither did the 'Marnemen'. The hard-pressed GIs had no wish to fight it out with some middle-aged cops, no matter how reluctant the latter were. Instead, they called up the 3rd's tank destroyers. The heavy vehicles fought their way through the rubble and, taking up position, started shelling the German policemen. The tank destroyers, with their massive 105mm cannon, made short work of the enemy police in their green uniforms and tall leather helmets and it didn't take long before the 140 policemen who had survived came clambering out of the rubble crying for mercy.

Still, O'Daniel was finding it hard to hold the ground he had captured. Overnight he turned his anti-tank companies into instant infantry and threw them into battle. They were 'bodies' and he needed bodies. Surprisingly enough, the transformed anti-tank gunners later won the coveted Presidential Unit Citation for their efforts in Nuremberg.

In the early hours of the morning of 19 April, while the fighting still raged in the centre of Nuremberg, Holz went to the office of the *Oberbürgermeister*, which was in a large air-raid shelter. For some reason Holz and Burgomaster Leibel started to argue, probably because Leibel wanted to surrender what was left of the city, and Holz wouldn't hear of it. In the anteroom outside, Leibel's staff could hear the *Gauleiter* ranting. Suddenly there was a single shot and then Holz stormed out of the office, leaving Leibel dead in his chair with a hole in the side of his head.

Had Leibel attempted to draw on Holz and been shot for his daring, or had the *Gauleiter* shot him in cold blood? Probably the latter. No one was ever to know. For Holz had only hours to live. He would never now report to his Führer that the city still held out.

Still the Americans' efforts to prepare the former *Adolf Hitler Platz* continued. The Brass were determined to enjoy their moment of triumph and capture the newspaper headlines back home. But to a disgusted Audie Murphy it all seemed so totally unnecessary. His comrades were dying for a city which had no strategic and little tactical value. In fact they were dying to help promote generals and for the 'prestige of the US Army'. As Murphy said to his postwar ghost writer, helping him with his 'autobiography', 'Spec, Nuremberg was simply a crock of shit.'*

* Spec McClure, who wrote most of Murphy's *To Hell and Back*, published in 1955.

V

WE SHALL HOLD OUT UNTIL THE
BRITISH KICK US IN THE ARSE

On Friday, 20 April, 1945, Hitler celebrated his fifty-sixth birthday in Berlin. Despite the terrible military situation, he was not particularly downcast. He even sipped a glass of champagne (*Sekt* of course) with the various notables who came to his bunker to congratulate him. He had already made his plans; in fact they had been finalized for over a week now. *Grossadmiral* Doenitz, the commander of the German Navy, whose submarines had nearly brought Britain to her knees in the winter of 1941/42, was to take over command in Northern Germany. The Führer himself would fly to his mountain retreat at Berchtesgaden and help supervise the battle from there. Ten days before, he had sent his servants on ahead to prepare the Berghof for his arrival. With them had fled frantic officials desperate to get out of Berlin while there was still time, and many of the *Prominenz*, Goering, Ribbentrop and the like, who were already deserting the sinking ship.

But that Friday afternoon when he went into the garden to pat the cheeks of twelve-year-old Hitler Youths who had been awarded the Iron Cross for bravery, he knew that he would remain in Berlin to die, 'in order to escape the shame of overthrow or capitulation', as he put it in his last Will and Testament. It was about then that he learned officially that Nuremberg had been captured by the Americans, which must have symbolized for him the end of the Reich. As Goebbels, who would soon die with Hitler in the bunker, expressed it somewhat obscurely,

'[We shall] hold out until the British kick us in the arse.' Little did he know that Friday that the British were in no position to kick anyone's arse.

At six-thirty that day, as Hitler received the last of his visitors, the 3rd Division's three regiments were drawn up in the former *Adolf Hitler Platz* to be addressed by the proud divisional general whose nickname it now bore. Standing under an improvised 'Old Glory', Iron Mike told his weary troops, 'We are standing on the site of the stronghold of Nazi resistance in our zone. Through your feats of arms, you have captured 4,000 prisoners and driven the Hun from every house and every castle and bunker in our part of Nuremberg. I congratulate you on your superior performance.' Now the other ceremonies followed, watched by a handful of bemused Germans who wondered what it was all about.

As Iron Mike was praising his soldiers Holz was fighting his last battle. At the local police headquarters, which still held out, Holz personally manned a machine gun, not against the enemy, but against the police, in order to prevent them from surrendering. But the cops' morale was broken. Holz thereupon decided to make a break for it before they surrendered. He and an SS officer who was prepared to go with him had spotted a hole in the wall of the courtyard which they thought wasn't covered by the Americans.

The SS officer made the first attempt. However, just as he was about to clamber through the hole, he was caught by a burst of machine-gun fire and fell to the ground dead.

That didn't stop Holz. Before the enemy machine gunner could re-aim, he dashed forward, struggled through the jagged shellhole and set off. But an American spotted him. A rifle cracked and Holz slammed back against the concrete, his jugular vein shattered. He was dead.

Eisenhower was in London when he heard the news of the fall of Nuremberg. He had been there for three days, sorting out problem after problem with Churchill and his military advisers. The news must have pleased him. It must have pleased him even more to know that Bavaria's capital city, Munich, the next in the path of the US 7th Army, was in the throes of a revolt. For the first and last time in the history of the 1,000 Year Reich, the German people had risen in arms against their brown-shirted masters.*

The time had come to do something about his current strategy for the last days of the war. As he wrote afterwards, 'Even before the Allied advance across central Germany began, we knew that the German Government was preparing to evacuate Berlin.' Now he knew that 'the continuation of the movement was no longer possible after Bradley's speedy advance barred further north–south traffic across the country. We knew also that Hitler had been unable to go south and that he was making his last stand in Berlin.'

Without the Führer, or any form of government, in the region of the Bavarian-Austrian Alps, what purpose would a leaderless Alpine Redoubt serve, even if it did exist?

It was a problem that Eisenhower finally swept under the carpet. Neither he nor any of his top generals ever gave a plausible explanation as to why their armies abandoned the 'glittering prize' of Berlin for the non-existent Alpine Redoubt. There was some talk by Bradley of the enormous casualties the US Army would incur, but that was about it. No one remarked on the fact that 'Eclipse' said that Berlin would be divided between the three main powers once it had been captured; and it was pretty clear from the Allied maps found with the 'Eclipse' document that it would fall to the Russians.

Eisenhower, seeming to have almost lost control of his vast armies, continued to allow them to advance due east through Germany to Austria, an advance which served no strategic or political purpose. Vienna, Austria's capital, had already been taken by the Red Army and by the end of the month the Russians would control all the capitals of Central Europe, from Belgrade, through Vienna, to Prague and finally up to Berlin. In essence the Russians had won the political victory, not only against the Germans, but also against their erstwhile allies, the Anglo-Americans.

---

* The revolt failed, just as the Nazi-inspired postwar werewolf movement did. Interestingly enough, alone of the occupied European countries, Germany failed to produce a long-standing resistance movement.

Surprisingly enough, amid all this uncertainty about the strategy of the final weeks, Eisenhower allowed Patton's Third Army to head for Prague, which was in a state of total confusion, with Czechs fighting Germans, Germans fighting both Russians and Czechs, and renegade Russians fighting all three. But Patton got only as far as Pilsen: 'I captured the goddam beer factories.' Here he was ordered to stop and let the Red Army take the capital itself.

So in this third week of April, 1945, while Eisenhower continued to discuss his plans with a disgruntled and disillusioned Churchill in London, his generals went on wasting many men's lives and resources capturing fortified German cities which had no value whatsoever. Indeed, by the end of that month the peak of military absurdity would be reached when two US divisions and one French raced each other for the 'honour' of capturing Hitler's mountain retreat, the Berghof, in the Bavarian Alps. Again it was all a matter of national prestige.

But, whether he liked it or not, on that Friday, 20 April, while Hitler celebrated his last birthday on this earth, Eisenhower was forced to face up to reality at last. He began to see that his new (and old, for that matter) strategy had been pointless. Now he was confronted not only by military problems, but political ones as well. These new problems, which he, and he alone, had to solve, occasioned by the imminent end of the war,* were twofold and in a way were interlinked. Moreover, both were concerned with America's erstwhile allies and both contained elements within them that might well lead to a new war in Europe.

For the first time since D-Day he was obliged to make his decisions single-handed. At last he was to be confronted with the dirty realities of European *Realpolitik*.

It had all started with de Gaulle's Free French. In the same week that Nuremberg fell General Patch had his 63rd, 100th and 44th Infantry Divisions, plus his 10th Armored Division, attacking towards Stuttgart. The drive for this key Swabian city had been supposedly co-ordinated with French General de

---

* By now President Roosevelt was dead and all decisions in Europe, military as well as political, were being made, in the main, by Eisenhower.

Lattre's 1st Army, coming up from the Black Forest after their belated crossing of the Rhine, days after the Anglo-American crossings.* According to the American planners, once Stuttgart had been taken it would be incorporated in the future US Zone of Occupation. It was something to which de Gaulle, always sensitive about matters concerning *la gloire de la France*, had given only tacit and temporary approval.

Unfortunately for the American planners, 'King Jean' (as the lordly de Lattre, who hated the English so much that he had volunteered to help the Germans in their planned invasion of Britain back in 1940, was known to his troops) had other ideas. Urged on by de Gaulle, the French First Army was driving all out for Stuttgart, burning and raping its way through the Black Forest towards the city. French prestige demanded that it should be taken by French arms and damn the Americans.

But the problem for Eisenhower was not confined to Stuttgart alone. Unknown to the French, their advance was endangering a highly secret US project, perhaps one of the most important of the war. Known as the 'Alsos Group', its job was to capture German scientists and material relating to German nuclear fission. By this time the team knew from documents captured at Strasbourg University that the remaining German centre for research into the production of a German atomic bomb was located at the small town of Hechingen, thirty-five miles south of Stuttgart. It had been planned that an Alsos team should accompany the fighting troops into Stuttgart and from there make a dash for Hechingen. For Eisenhower had ordered that on no account should the German scientists and their research data fall into French hands. Just like his political masters in Washington, he wanted the atom bomb, at the time being tested for later use in Japan, to remain a monopoly of the Anglo-Americans.

* The first French soldiers crossed the Rhine in a single rowing boat, all eleven of them, and all save one African troops. While today nothing remains to remind one of the massive Anglo-American assault on the river, a weathered stone near the city of Speyer commemorates the pathetically small French 'assault'. In the end Patch took pity on the French and lent them some bridging equipment.

So while General Devers, head of the US 6th Army Group, to which the 7th Army belonged, blustered and threatened to cut off de Lattre's supplies if he didn't relinquish Stuttgart which he had just captured, Eisenhower tried to cool the situation. On Churchill's advice he wrote to de Gaulle, deploring de Lattre's defiance of Devers (who also had overall command of the First French Army), but stating that he, personally, did not want to see supplies cut off from the French Army.

Behind the scenes, however, there was near panic at Supreme Headquarters, and in Washington Secretary of War Stimson personally agreed a plan with General Marshall called 'Operation Harborage'. It envisaged a reinforced US Army Corps, consisting of the US 13th Airborne Division and the 10th Armored, cutting right through the French zone of operations and taking Hechingen whether de Lattre liked it or not.

Wiser heads prevailed. Under the command of a Colonel Boris Pash, the Alsos team, reinforced by the US Army combat engineers and British specialists, crossed French territory without permission and made contact with the German atomic specialists who proved all too willing to leave with their 'captors', and the team started to withdraw. When they ran into French roadblocks, Pash somehow talked his way through. But one French officer was not convinced and thought the Americans were after Marshal Pétain and the Vichy Government, which had worked hand-in-glove with the Germans and which was now located just down the road at Sigmaringen. Finally Pash convinced him that this was not the case, but, to be on the safe side, he tricked the French into keeping out of the way by saying that the area was soon to be subjected to a heavy bombardment by American artillery.

It turned out that the German bomb was in no way as advanced as the American one, but Germans such as Werner von Braun, the man whose V2s had killed or injured some 16,000 Londoners that winter, were soon on their way to America to begin the new battle – against the Russians.

VI

I DON'T UNDERSTAND WHY THE PM HAS BEEN SO DETERMINED TO INTERMINGLE POLITICAL AND MILITARY CONSIDERATIONS

Even with the atom bomb crisis resolved the French Army in Germany continued to worry Eisenhower, and, naturally, Marshal as well. As Eisenhower told Marshal Juin, another senior French officer who had only gone over to the Allies when it seemed they were likely to win the war, 'If I can no longer count with certainty on the operational use of French forces, I will have to recommend to the Combined Chiefs of Staff that they shouldn't equip any new French forces.' It was a decidedly unveiled threat. The French knew that if they wanted to reclaim their rebellious colonies in Africa and Asia after the war they would need to build up a modern army. This they could only do with the aid of the United States.*

But the threat seemed to have no effect on de Gaulle, and hardly had the problem in Stuttgart been solved before a new one arose. On the Franco-Italian border the French Army started taking over Italian territory which Eisenhower had previously

---

* In June, 1945, the division to which the author belonged was alerted for immediate action against the French Army in Syria, which had refused to stop the bombing of Damascus. One month after the end of the Second World War in Europe the French, seemingly, had become so troublesome that the powers that be in Washington and London were prepared to fight their erstwhile allies.

102

agreed to give back to his 'co-belligerents', the Italians. As the latter had fought against the Anglo-American forces till September, 1943, they could hardly be called allies. So they became, in the jargon of the time, 'co-belligerents'. Now the Italians complained to the Supreme Commander and Eisenhower had to step in and threaten to cut off supplies to the First French Army. De Lattre backed off, but threatened reprisals. Eisenhower knew by now what those reprisals would be – the denial of the vital supply ports and the severance of the vast communications infrastructure that ran through France to the front in Germany. As yet the US Army didn't have a single port in Germany to take the place of Marseilles or Cherbourg. As for Antwerp, in Belgium, that was reserved for the British.

Now, with Churchill's agreement, Eisenhower decided that the alternative sanctioned by Roosevelt the previous year should have priority. Bremen should be captured at once, so that the Bremen-Bremerhaven port complex in the future British Zone of Occupation could become the American Army's main source of supply from the States. General de Gaulle would then no longer be in a position to blackmail the Americans.

But there was more to come. The French were not the only potential trouble-makers; there was also 'Uncle Joe' Stalin to be reckoned with. Contrary to previous agreements with the Anglo-Americans, he now seemed to be laying claim to the whole of Eastern and Central Europe. His motto appeared to be: whatever the Red Army captures, it keeps.

And it didn't end there. The Red Army seemed hell-bent on infringing upon what had hitherto been thought to be a British sphere of influence. The communists were fomenting trouble and, in one case, downright civil war in France, Belgium, Italy and Greece. Churchill, Eisenhower's host in London in those last days of April, 1945, now wondered what were the objectives of those Red Army units who had bypassed Berlin to the north and were heading for the River Elbe. Would they stop when they reached the British lines on the other side of the river, as had been agreed under the terms of 'Eclipse'?

As Churchill wrote to his Foreign Secretary, Anthony Eden, on 19 April, 'Our arrival at Lübeck [which would seal off

Schleswig-Holstein] before our friends from Stettin should save a lot of argument later on. There is no reason why Russia should occupy Denmark, which is a country to be liberated and have its sovereignty restored. Our position at Lübeck, if we get it, would be decisive in this matter.'

Abruptly Eisenhower seemed to realize that his strategy since March had been ineffectual. He had accepted what the commander of the US 82nd Airborne Division, General 'Slim Jim' Gavin, had called the 'Bradley Plan' back in the first week of March, 1945. Gavin, as concerned with US prestige as the next, had stated bluntly what that plan was: '[It] would obviate the need to give American divisions to Montgomery and [relegated] Montgomery and his Army Group to a secondary rôle.'

The result had been that Eisenhower had neglected the political objective, which at this stage had become more important than the military ones. He had handed Central Europe over to the Russians on a plate, while his armies had battered their heads against a series of fortified cities. Their capture had gained the US Army and its generals the prestige they craved for, but little else of any importance in the postwar world – and the cost in lives had been prohibitive. Patton's Third Army alone evacuated 135,000 casualties by air in the last four weeks of the war.

During this time Montgomery's British Army Group had played the rôle of an unimportant flank guard to the US armies – a flank guard against what, one might have asked. In Holland the remnants of the German Army trapped there were starving like the local populace and were already negotiating for peace with the Allies. In the north, under the command of Grand Admiral Doenitz, a million-odd German troops were still fighting a strictly defensive battle, aimed at allowing as many Germans as possible, both soldiers and civilians, to flee westwards in front of the advancing Russians. In essence, through Bradley's and Patton's influence, the British had been relegated to an unimportant sideshow to the north while they waited for the Americans to finish the war for them. Now all that was about to change.

Suddenly it was the British who had been at fault all along. As Eisenhower told Field Marshal Alan Brooke, he had urged Montgomery to greater efforts in his drive from the Rhine to the north of Germany all along. Brooke should know that Eisenhower 'had done everything that is humanly possible for me to do and . . . I have not been merely giving lip service to an idea without doing anything to implement it.' At that three-day conference in London Eisenhower told Brooke that he had formed a reserve for Montgomery's use. Now he washed his hands of responsibility for any further delays on the Field Marshal's part.

At the end of the conference Eisenhower and his PR man, Commander Butcher, returned to Telegraph Cottage outside the capital, which had been his retreat with his mistress, Kay Summersby, before the Invasion. On the way there he told Butcher that he had grown 'quite fond of the old man'. Often Churchill had seen him off in his 'slippers and dressing gown', a sure sign that he regarded him as a good friend. All the same, he would now cable Marshall about the latest decisions made in London. Part of that signal read, 'I don't quite understand why the Prime Minister has been so determined to intermingle political and military considerations'!

That was the way in which the fate of Central Europe was being decided in the spring of 1945.

Four days before, Montgomery had signalled to the War Office from Germany: 'The formations of the 21st Army Group are nearly all getting very tired. They have been fighting continuously since 8 February and operations across the Elbe to the area Lübeck-Kiel will probably go very slowly.'

Now, on Friday, 20 April Eisenhower informed Montgomery that there had been a radical change of plan. Montgomery's flank guard mission had been given top priority. He was to be given, with immediate effect, Major-General Ridgway's XVIII US Airborne Corps, six divisions strong and including some of the most experienced divisions in the US Army, plus the British 6th Airborne, which had recently suffered heavy casualties during the Rhine drop in March. More to the point, to ensure fast movement – for Montgomery had only one armoured division, the British 17th Armoured, on the Elbe front – the Ridgway corps included the veteran US 7th Armored Division.*

This new corps would ensure that the British 2nd Army reached the Baltic in the Lübeck-Wismar area before the Russians did and effectively seal off the Schleswig-Holstein peninsula and Denmark. Meanwhile Montgomery could concentrate on his drive on Bremen, which now, to Montgomery's quiet surprise, was of such great importance to Eisenhower.

Although he was always quick enough to criticize American military leadership, Montgomery never had any complaints about American troops, as long as they were under *his* command. He welcomed Ridgway's XVIII Corps with open arms and set about planning his usual set-piece attack, this time on Bremen.

As he explained the plan to the War Office's military secretary, Major-General 'Simbo' Simpson: 'Battle for Bremen is to be fought by 30 Corps. 43, 51 and 3 British Divs will attack Bremen south and west of R. Weser, while 52 Div north of this river is to come in at Bremen from the east . . . Assault on Bremen will be either on 23 or 24 April.

'Simultaneously with battle for Bremen or just after it, Canadian Army is to clear up the Wilhelmshaven-Emden peninsula. Canadian Army will probably leave only one division in East Holland while this is going on. Meanwhile the Second Army will be closing up to R.Elbe.'

But although a whole US corps was on its way to help him cross the Elbe before the drive northwards to the Baltic, Montgomery, at that moment, had only the three divisions of the British 8 Corps to carry out the crossing. Most of his infantry, as we have seen, plus the Guards Armoured Division, would be involved in the battle for Bremen. For this reason Montgomery was hesitant about giving a definite date for the assault crossing of the river east of Hamburg, the siege of which was already taking up part of two precious divisions. As he wrote to Brooke at the time, 'If opposition is not severe, the crossing may take

* Only four months before, Montgomery had rescinded an order given by Ridgway and thus probably saved the US 7th Armored from destruction in the Battle of the Bulge. See C. Whiting, *The Last Assault* for details.

place on night 20/21 April. If, as it seems likely, there is strong opposition and a staged assault has to take place, it will probably not be until about a week after Bremen.'

Without the resources of the US 9th Army, which Eisenhower had taken away from him the previous month at Bradley's instigation, Montgomery didn't have enough engineers and bridging equipment to conduct a battle for the fortified seaport *and* undertake an assault crossing of the Elbe against determined opposition.

All the same, with the limited resources at his disposal, Montgomery was prepared to have a go. He had seen the British Army break down and flee at Dunkirk, with his own Corps Commander and future mentor, Brooke, sobbing broken-heartedly on his skinny shoulder. He had lived through those black years of defeat upon defeat until his own victory at El Alamein, when a depressed Churchill had declared of the British soldier, 'When will he ever begin to fight?'

Now once again Montgomery had a chance of glory, which he desired so fervently. The demeaning rôle, as he saw it, which the Americans had allotted him had been changed overnight. Now he was no longer to play flank guard to Bradley's Army Group. Instead he had been given a major military objective, one which had important political implications for the postwar world. Finally, after five long years, he was in a position to avenge that terrible defeat of 1940 when the German Army had run the British out of Europe.

Victories at Lübeck and Bremen would set the seal on his own reputation. They would make him a worthy successor of Britain's greatest ever soldier. He, who had won the Battle of El Alamein, would follow in the footsteps of the Duke of Wellington. Little did he know then how great that victory was to be.

BOOK TWO

BLOODY BREMEN

'All conditions are more calculable, all
obstacles are more surmountable, than
those of human resistance.'

Sir Basil Liddell Hart

1

15 APRIL

I

HIER IST BREMEN

Urged on by their Divisional Commander, General 'Butcher' Thomas, who didn't bother about losses, the men of the 43rd Wessex Division pushed ever closer to the river line. For days his infantry battalions, in some cases reduced from 800 men to a mere 200 after three solid weeks of relentless conflict, had been fighting their way closer to Bremen. Now, on the evening of Saturday 14th April, they had reached the line of the first of the three rivers covering the city, the River Leithe. Here, just short of their objective, the crossroads at the German town of Ahlhorn, they waited for their next orders.

The lead company of the 1st Worcestershire Regiment knew that they wouldn't have to wait on the banks of the river for long. Thomas would see to that.

A veteran of the First World War, in which he had been decorated for bravery, Ivor Thomas, commander of the 43rd Infantry Division, was brave but wooden. The result was that by the end of the war he had run up a butcher's bill of 12,484 casualties, a virtual turnround in the Division's strength, with one brigadier and twelve battalion or regimental commanders killed in action and another seven wounded.

That Saturday Thomas fumed as he waited for the CO of the 1st Worcesters to do something about crossing the Leithe. The bridge was blown, the opposite bank was steep and slick with mud and there were mines everywhere. It was going to be a tough assignment for the exhausted, depleted infantry.

In the event it was the Germans who took the initiative. At 5.45, just after dawn, the rumble of artillery, the ever-present background music to war, started to rise in volume. As Major

Peter Hall, a company commander, recalled after the war, 'There was a tremendous barrage on my forward platoons . . . From my Coy HQ I saw our forward platoon soldiers running back.'

Major Hall tried to reorganize his first line of defence, but just then his two company signallers were killed by a shell. 'The wireless was destroyed . . . The only link was through the Regimental wireless network of the 13th/18th Hussars. We were on our own!'

An enemy Royal Tiger started to rumble through the wood to the infantry's front. It snapped off the thin pines like matchwood. Someone tried to tackle it with a PIAT, but the bomb simply bounced off the tank's armour. Behind it and the other tanks, the infantry came in their *trauben* (grapes), the standard German attack formation for infantry with tanks. They came cautiously, weapons clutched to their hips, trying to keep to the shelter of the tanks for as long as possible. And all the time, the 'massive artillery thunder', as Major Hall called it, continued.

The German attack was speeding up, as here and there a young German officer from the mixed Second Marine Infantry Division and the 12th SS Training and Replacement Battalion shouted an order or fired off a burst from his Schmeisser. The Worcesters' line erupted into action. Rifles cracked and Bren guns rattled away. Major Hall called for everyone who could hold and fire a rifle to join in. If they didn't, the Germans would soon overrun the lads of the 1st Worcesters. The boys rallied the best they could. Even the cooks took up the challenge.

'D' Company broke as some of the Worcesters clambered out of their pits and began to pull back. Their Company Commander, Major Elder, was hit and went down. His second-in-command, Captain Percy Huxter, took over. A shell whistled through his HQ without exploding and that did it. The Captain grabbed a PIAT and, followed by his HQ staff, went 'tank-bashing'.

Now it was the turn of the Germans to falter. But their young officers, brutalized by the bitter battles on the *Ostfront* in Russia, rallied them with threats. Then the two-hour battle, the last real one the Worcesters would fight in their eleven-month campaign since Normandy, began to peter out. The attackers had lost a

Royal Tiger Tank, a large number of prisoners and between 400 and 600 dead.

The Worcesters had also had enough. They had lost many good men since Normandy and didn't want to lose any more now that the end of the war was close. An appeal went out to the 43rd's Divisional Artillery Commander. He relayed it to XXX Corps Artillery Commander, the corps to which the Wyvern men belonged. For days now ammunition had been coming forward by the truckload. But demands for a 'shoot' had been few. Now the whole weight of the Corps artillery fell upon the German attackers. That did it. Those still on their feet fled or surrendered, leaving the woods full of their dead.

Major Hall was confronted by fifty-odd Germans ready to give themselves up. One of them approached him and asked in perfect English, 'Where do you live in England? I spent five years at Oxford before the war.' Hall's reply, he said later, was unprintable.

At five-thirty that Sunday afternoon the 1st Worcesters, together with the 7th Somerset Light Infantry, started to advance again as timid old German men and women appeared from the shattered woods on both sides of the road. Using sign language, the peasants asked if they could collect the German dead in the little wooden *böllerwagen* they towed behind them and bury them elsewhere. The Worcesters' officers gave their approval and the old folk started to gather up the dead. 'It was a sombre scene,' Brigadier Essame of the 43rd Division recalled after the war, 'pathetic in its utter futility, even to the battle-hardened troops of the Division.'

But there was little time for the Worcesters and the SLI to reflect on the futility of war. For them the battle had to go on. They headed for the Ahlhorn crossroads which led to the larger cities of Oldenburg and Wilhelmshaven on the coast. It was a classic attack. Under a rolling barrage provided by the Shermans of the 13th/18th Hussars and 'a pepper-pot shoot' from the supporting heavy machine guns and mortars the soldiers of the rural south-west advanced.

The lead platoon advanced across the flat German fields, broken at regular intervals by the irrigation ditches typical of that part of North Germany. The German defenders had been told that Ahlhorn boasted a military airfield and had been ordered to hold it because it was to be used by the new jets which could shoot anything out of the sky. So they crouched in their pits, which might well serve as their graves before long.

Then machine guns hissed as the infantry emerged from the smokescreen put down by the Hussars. They doubled forward and minutes later it was all over. Here and there a German was too slow in raising his hands and got the butt of a rifle for his lack of speed. Prisoners started to come forward in ever-growing numbers.

But the victory had to be paid for. As the others advanced, some Wyvern men stayed behind with their dead comrades. They took off their helmets and, digging their rifles, bayonet-first, in the soft soil, placed the helmets on the rifle butts to mark the spot. Then the man's AB 64 and Paybook were removed for identification purposes, while the lower of the two identity discs round the man's throat was ripped off and thrust inside his mouth (again for later identification purposes) and the lips firmly pressed together. Finally the eyelids were closed and it was all over for one young man. A few days hence the telegraph boy would cycle up to his home with the buff standard communication which began: 'The War Office regrets to inform you . . .'

7 Platoon, under Sergeant Harry Carroll of the Somerset Light Infantry, fought its way into Ahlhorn itself. The young men rushed the telephone exchange and captured it without loss. They were out to 'organize' – as the jargon of the time described looting – souvenirs. All the same they were wary of booby traps. The NCO's gaze fell on two electric sockets. One was labelled 'Bremen' in black handwriting. He hesitated. Was this kind of some booby trap? Finally he gave in to his curiosity. He plugged in the other socket and summoned up his skimpy German vocabulary.

'*Wer da, bitte?*' he asked.

Then, faintly but distinctly, a female voice answered, '*Hier ist Bremen.*'

Montgomery's armies had made their first contact with their objective. Bremen was only a matter of miles away now.

II

AN EPISODE WHICH
SHOCKED THE WORLD

On that Sunday, 15 April, with the Second World War in Europe still to continue for another three weeks, there was no rest for the British or the Canadians. Advancing northwards up the corridor formed by the River Ems to the west and the River Weser to the east, for them it was a confused day. There were moments of brutality going hand in hand with moments of intense relief, even happiness.

The Canadians – every man a volunteer, for their country would not sanction conscripted men going overseas* – were running out of soldiers fast. Still they fought on bravely. But there was a bitterness among them, not helped by their excessive drinking and, at least by British Army standards, lack of discipline, which led to excesses.

On the previous Saturday Lieutenant-Colonel Wigle, the CO of the Canadian Argyll and Sutherland Highlanders belonging to the Canadian 2nd Corps, had been killed in a firefight just outside his own HQ in the small town of Friesoythe. Now on this 'day of peace', the Colonel's men decided to take revenge. They were certain that Colonel Wigle had been shot by a German sniper dressed in civilian clothes.

Four days before, when other Canadians thought they had been fired on by German soldiers in civilian clothes or actual civilians themselves during the battle for the small town of

* During the first attempt to send conscripts overseas to Europe most of the men jumped ship and deserted.

117

Soegel where OSS agent Kappius had dropped the previous year, they had sent in their engineers after the place had been captured. Then, after turfing out the inhabitants at bayonet point, the engineers set about systematically burning down the whole place!

Now Wigle's men did the same at Friesoythe. The civilians were booted out and then the fire-raisers began their deadly work. Some of the Germans pleaded to take, at least, one treasured possession with them, but the angry Canadians weren't having it. They were not allowed to take anything with them – and those were orders! Then the Canadians went from house to house and set them alight.

At the far end of the line of five divisions now heading for Bremen, the Seaforths of the 51st Highland Division had settled in at the Lower Saxon village of Holzminden. The men of the 'Highway Decorators', so named after the divisional patch 'HD' and their fondness for plastering it along every 'highway',* thought they might have a couple of days away from the war there – which they did. But the war followed them in a different fashion. The Seaforths' HQ was plagued by the local minister of religion, 'a cadaverous earnest soul,' who came to complain 'every hour' in fractured English about the deprivations of the freed Czechs, Poles, Russians, French and Lithuanians who roamed Holzminden doing exactly what they liked. Invariably he tagged his own personal request onto every complaint, with 'Is it possible that I may have permission out of the town? I desire to visit my home. It is incended.'

The minister was boring, but not as bad as the local baker. 'He had a Hitler moustache,' one of the Seaforth officers said. 'The first time we saw him he walked into the office, as if he owned it [he did; it was his house], tossed up a Nazi salute, walked to a chair and without a by your leave made himself at home.'

This behaviour incurred the wrath of the Seaforths' Jewish sergeant. He made inquiries about the baker among the

---

* The author remembers visiting Libya a few years ago and seeing the big red HD of the 51st painted on ruined Italian and Arab dwellings the whole length of the coastal road to Tripoli. Perhaps they are still there.

displaced persons and discovered that the baker was a dyed-in-the-wool Nazi.

'On the morning [before the Seaforths left for their next battle] Sergeant Schlatts came back with two Russians who led the baker to a spot in the garden. They dug. They unearthed a pistol and a rifle, both well greased.' The baker's fate was sealed. As a Seaforth officer who saw the digging-up of the weapons commented after the war, 'I don't know what happened to the baker after he was led way. He was shot I suppose.'

There were a lot of German civilians who had terrorized their foreign workers in the Nazi period and now ended up being beaten to death or, if they were lucky, lined up against a wall and shot.

But the suffering was not one-sided. Colonel Crozier of the Manchester Regiment noted in his diary of the 53rd Welsh Division: '158 and 160 Brigades are just played out. Some battalions are less than 200 strong and they are very tired.' In fact the infantry of Montgomery's attacking divisions, many containing up to forty percent teenage replacements, were exhausted and badly depleted. On that Sunday when the 53rd's Welch Regiment were asked to find a detachment to guard a recently captured bridge at Weitzmühlen, they literally couldn't find sufficient men to do the job.

The men of the 1/5th Welch had suffered heavy losses during the fighting since the breakout from the Rhine bridgehead. For five days they, and other troops of the Division, had been engaged in a battle to capture the bridge across the River Aller at Rethem. The first probe had ended in disaster with only twenty-four men returning. Brigadier Wilsey of the 53rd, directing the operation, now ordered up two companies, to be covered by three whole regiments of artillery, while the Welch's sister regiments, the 7th Royal Welch Fusiliers and the East Lancs, attacked on the flanks.

Again disaster. The SS and the Marines defending Rethem were waiting for them. One company was virtually wiped out. Tanks succumbed to the German anti-tank guns at point blank range and twenty-three unfortunate fusiliers were captured, wounded or killed. They were to be the first of many.

Now the Welch attacked for forty-eight hours without sleep and little food. As the adjutant, Captain Cuthbertson, noted at the time, 'A number of our new reinforcements were very young and quickly became exhausted. It was the only time that I observed soldiers sleeping standing up, leaning on their rifles.'

The Battalion was in an appalling condition. In those forty-eight hours the 1/5th Welch had lost seven officers and 186 other ranks, with the supporting battalions on both flanks suffering about the same number.

Encouraged by their ability to hold up a whole British brigade, the boys of the *Hitler Youth*, some, according to their grave-stones, as young as 16, plus the Marines hastily converted into infantrymen, counter-attacked. They infiltrated into the farm buildings held by the battalion HQ. As Major 'Zonk' Lewis recalled after the war, 'The enemy started shooting up the transport and Coy HQ with panzerfaust.' With the farm buildings blazing all around him, Lewis ordered the survivors to make a dash for it. They were to run to a building a hundred yards away where they would reorganize. Hardly had he given the order when a shed containing the battalion's reserve ammunition went up with a roar. Around them other buildings began to collapse. Then the men went beserk and lit into the German marines with fists and feet. 'There is no etiquette in war,' as Major Lewis added.

But the diversion paid off. 'Simultaneously, all those who had been taken prisoner turned on their captors and before long the enemy dead included two officers, neither of whom had a bullet wound on them. The enemy learned by experience what a British soldier could do to them with his fists and hands. The enemy melted away, leaving their dead.'

Their comrades trying desperately to hang on in the now re-captured Rethem were not so fortunate. The Hitler Youth SS caught the defenders off guard as they swept down the main street from the river, firing from the hip and setting the houses on both sides alight. In an hour the Welshmen had suffered a staggering fifty per cent casualties. But they held on as best they could until the SS manhandled a quick-firing 20mm cannon into place and started pounding the remaining British-held houses.

It was too much for the survivors, many of them wounded and

most of them green reinforcements. They began to fling away their weapons and raise their arms in surrender. At this late stage of the war even the toughest and most steadfast didn't want to throw away their lives for the sake of this God-forsaken German town.

One of the Welch, however, decided he was not going to go into the bag with the rest. He was Private Parry and he lay in the débris-littered gutter, feigning death, as the jubilant young SS men rounded up their prisoners, searching them for cigarettes and chocolate.

According to Parry's own story, which he told to the Press later, fifteen of his comrades were dragged out of a burning house and lined up against a wall. One of their captors then picked up an abandoned British Bren gun and let loose, firing cold-bloodedly into the British PoWs. They fell in a row and the murderer then dropped the gun and crossed to where Parry was feigning death 25 yards away. He kicked him in the ribs, but fortunately his ammunition pouch deadened the pain, enabling him to prevent himself from yelling out in pain.

Satisfied that all the Tommies were dead, the SS left with their booty. After a tense half-hour, making sure that the Germans had really gone, Parry stole back to his own lines and told his story of the 'Massacre at Rethem'.

One of the press correspondents present was particularly interested. He knew all about the 'Hitler Youth Division' (the 12th SS Panzer). Already they had been involved in one massacre, involving Canadians taken prisoner during the battle for Caen. Indeed the Division's commander at that time was in Allied custody, waiting trial for war crimes. General Kurt Meyer, known as 'Panzermeyer', would be soon sentenced to death for the shooting of those Canadians. Now the Hitler Youth were up to their old games once more.

The pressman's name was Captain Brian de Grineau of the *Illustrated London News* and he started sketching a picture of what Parry had just told him of the events in Rethem. On 21 April, 1945, it appeared as the centrefold of that old-fashioned weekly. On the left of the picture is a large, double-roofed barn and at the foot of it stand some dozen defiant British soldiers, all unarmed, with their back to the wall. Above the drawing was

121

the headline: 'Defiant Welshmen Being Mown Down in Sweeps of Gun'. In the centre a burly, helmeted SS man with a Bren gun at his hip carries out the murder. Another caption reads: 'SS Executioner with Captured Bren Gun. Lest we forget. The Massacre of Welsh Prisoners at Rethem. An Episode Which Shocked the World'.

In fact Private Parry's tale was a total fabrication, another of those unfounded rumours such as that which had occasioned the Canadian Argyll and Sutherland Highlanders to burn down Friescoythe on that Sunday. For reasons known only to Parry, who was soon dispatched to the rear never to reappear, he had invented the story of the 'Massacre at Rethem'*. When the 1/5th Welch and 7th Royal Welch Fusiliers finally did take the town they found the 'massacre victims' safely tucked away in local hospitals being tended for by German doctors and nurses. As the historian of the Manchester Regiment records: 'The Germans had scrupulously observed the rules of war.'

But Private Parry's tale had its effect. The news of the 'Rethem Massacre' spread rapidly throughout the troops of the 'British Liberation Army'. Some divisions, such as the Seventh Armoured, featured the affair in their official newspaper for the troops. But mostly it was transmitted along the military grapevine.

* A survey of casualties in the British 2nd Army after the crossing of the Rhine concluded that nearly 20 per cent of them were caused by 'combat stress'. Perhaps Parry was 'bomb-happy' when he made up his story.

III

EXCUSE ME, SIR, BUT DR KLEIN
WISHES TO BE SHOT, SIR

The 'Massacre at Rethem' increased the vengeful mood of the soldiers. It didn't need General Eisenhower's new 'Non-Fraternization Ban'* to make the troops steer clear of the enemy. In the last three weeks of the war it had to be a very nippy German soldier who surrendered successfully.

Outside Hamburg the 1/5th Queens and the Devons, its sister battalion of the Seventh Armoured Division, the 'Desert Rats', were dug in on a wooded slope near the German hamlet of Vahrendorf. One of the Queens, a rakish-looking captain with an MC, was just writing home to his wife: 'For the last three days we haven't advanced an inch. We are in defence and the Boches on our front are very aggressive. Sometimes I begin to think I should have joined another regiment because somehow or other the Queens always seemed to attract all the Nazi fanatics on its front.'

The future newspaper magnate Robert Maxwell (as he was now calling himself) paused, just in time to hear the small-arms fire as the SS attacked down the hill once again. Hastily he scribbled, 'Shooting has just started. My platoon is being attacked. I must go.'

What happened next in the battle between the Queens and

---

* This stated that the troops should have no dealings with the Germans, on pain of punishment, save on official business. The only exceptions were children under eight. As the troops quipped, 'The little girls are very big for their age here, and they *do* love fags and chocs.'

the Devons and their teenage SS assailants still remains shrouded in secrecy. But we can guess. In the end the SS were beaten off, seventy-odd SS men were taken prisoner and the firing stopped. But not for long. Alerted by another long burst of small-arms fire, one of the few civilians who had remained in the hamlet, Frau Witt, came out of the cellar where she had sheltered during the battle. She didn't get far. A British corporal armed with a Sten gun soon ordered her to return to her cottage. Then, seeing she was just an inquisitive old woman, he laughed and pointed to a freshly smoking shell crater as if that was explanation enough.Short-sightedly she peered into it. It was filled with the bodies of dead SS men. 'Twenty of them,' Frau Witt thought she heard the corporal say before she decided that it was safer to return to her cottage. Later, after a twenty-two-hour curfew, the civilians were allowed to go about their business once more and during the course of the day found forty-two more bodies of SS men, buried in a common grave, eighteen of whom were never identified.*

Whatever had happened at that little hamlet – for the truth of that almost forgotten 'massacre', if such it was, will never be known now – the events there were typical of the new brutalization of some British soldiers in Germany.

But there was worse to come. On the same Sunday that the Germans launched their last major counter-attacks on the advancing British troops of the 2nd Army Brigadier Churcher's 159th Brigade of the 11th Armoured Division were surprised by two German officers approaching their lines. For a few moments before the officers, both bearing white flags, were brought in, the men thought this was the start of the great German surrender which they had been expecting for days now.

The two officers were taken to the HQ of Brigadier Churcher, but he was to be disappointed. This wasn't to be the start of the mass surrender. Instead they asked only for a local surrender. They reported that, immediately to the 11th Division's front,

* Today they are interred not far from the hamlet's Kiekeberg Mountain. Fifty years on, members of an ex-servicemen's organization visit the site every year to pay tribute to the dead, who, they maintain, were 'shot in cold blood after being taken prisoner at the orders of a crazed blood-thirsty British NCO.'

there was some sort of prison camp which was filled with seriously ill civilians who were not allowed to leave the place in case they spread the typhus which apparently raged there and the Germans were prepared to withdraw from the area so that there would be no fighting around the camp.

Churcher contacted his boss, General 'Pip' Roberts, the youngest divisional commander in the British Army, and Roberts, eager to continue his drive to the Elbe, in his turn got in touch with his chief, the Corps Commander, 'Bubbles' Barker. Barker agreed to a forty-eight-hour truce and the guns of the 11th Armoured Division fell silent for the first time in weeks as the first British units set off to find the camp. It had two names, but it would go down in history by its second one – Belsen.

Up front with the tanks of the 23rd Hussars, Captain Derrick Sington, a former journalist and linguist, was in command of Loudspeaker Unit One – two men and a van equipped with a battery of enormous loudspeakers. It would be the job of the three German-speakers in the unit to make the first announcement to the inmates of this strange camp which apparently presented a danger to friend and foe alike.

Driving with the tanks up the dead-straight road between the dripping pines Sington's nostrils were assailed by a strange and nauseating odour which he could not identify. Later Sington wrote: 'It reminded me of the entrance to a zoo. We came into the smell of ordure – like the smell of a monkey house.' They were approaching the greatest charnel house in Western Europe, one whose name would survive long after most of those there that April day were dead.

Sington turned off the main road, drove down a smaller one to the left and stopped by a red and white pole. There stood a group of immaculately uniformed German and Hungarian officers, led by a powerful-looking *Hauptsturmführer* of the *Allgemeine SS** With a scar across one cheek. Later the British would learn that he was the infamous Josef Kramer, the Camp Commandant. The enemy officers saluted. Sington got down

---

* General SS, to distinguish from the fighting branch of the Black Guards, the Armed SS (*Waffen SS*).

from the cab and said in German, 'I propose to go in and make a loudspeaker announcement.'

Kramer frowned. 'They're calm now,' he said. 'It would be unwise to risk a tumult.'

Sington ignored the remark and ordered Kramer to open the gate. The SS officer was visibly taken aback and said, 'I can't do that without authority from the *Wehrmacht* commandant.'

Again Sington ignored him. 'Stand on the running board,' he ordered. 'You have to guide us round the camp, stopping at suitable points to make loudspeaker announcements.'

Minutes later Sington was shocked beyond measure by what he saw. On all sides were starving, dead and dying prisoners in lice-ridden, faeces-stained striped pyjamas – men, women, children, dragged from their homes over half of Europe and brought to this dread place in what had once been a tourist resort for the citizens of Hamburg and Bremen. 'Now the tumult is beginning,' Kramer said in alarm.

At that moment a panicked German soldier started firing over the shaven heads of the crowd surging forward to the loudspeaker van. Sington drew his own revolver and shouted at the wild-eyed *landser* to stop firing at once – or else.

Then, as Sington wrote afterwards, 'Suddenly a dozen striped figures jumped into the crowd, hitting again and again with sticks and packing-case strips bending double with the impetus of the blows they struck.'

These were the dreaded *Kapos*, prisoners themselves, but mostly German and belonging to the organized communist bands within the camps. The SS didn't need to bother themselves about the inner camps. The *Kapos* just kept order for them for better rations and the promise that they wouldn't be sent to their deaths.

So enraged was Sington by the sight of the *Kapos* beating their fellow prisoners that he cried angrily, 'The Germans have nothing more to do with this camp. The camp is now under the control of the British Army.' As if to emphasize the change of role, Sington pointed to an inmate dying on a pallet of straw and yelled at Kramer, 'Pick up that man and take him to the hospital.'

Surprisingly, Kramer, the master of death for so long, did what he was told. By the time the camp was burned to the ground by the British Army, he would be begging to be allowed to die. But that was later. On that day, the Sunday of Liberation, eight hundred human beings died in Belsen.

The infamy of Belsen put Montgomery and his troops back in the news once more. They had been virtually forgotten since their crossing of the Rhine over three weeks before, but now the British arrival at Belsen attracted the war correspondents once more and they came swarming up from the press camps in Brussels, Paris and Luxembourg. Christopher Buckley, Alan Moorehead and, perhaps the most famous one of them all, Ed Murrow, were all there. One of them, Leonard Mosley, reported: 'The British soldiers who took over Belsen looked around and what they saw made them mad with rage. They beat the SS guards and set them to collecting the bodies of the dead, keeping them always at the double; back and forth they went all day long always running, men and women alike, from death pile to death pit, with the stringy remains of their victims over their shoulders. When one of them dropped to the ground with exhaustion, he was beaten with a rifle butt. When another stopped for a break, she was kicked until she ran again, or prodded with a bayonet to the accompaniment of lewd shouts and laughs. When one tried to escape or disobeyed an order, he was shot.'

When another correspondent arrived at the camp and was being briefed by a senior officer, a sergeant came up, saluted and snapped without a trace of emotion in his voice, 'Excuse me, sir, but Dr Klein wishes to be shot, sir.' Dr Klein was a member of Kramer's staff.

Alan Moorehead, the Australian correspondent of the *Daily Express*, who since 1940 had seen more fighting than most soldiers, was invited by an army captain to see Dr Klein die. 'He's a nice specimen,' the captain said. 'He invented some of the tortures here. He used to go round the huts saying, "Too many people here. Far too many." Then he used to loose off his revolver round the hut. The doctor had just finished being inter-rogated.'

Some interrogation! A sergeant opened the door to his cell and bellowed, 'Come on, get up.'

Klein was lying in his own blood, a massive figure with a large head and scruffy beard. He heaved himself half-upright by the back of a chair. When he was on his feet he flung his arms open to his repelled visitors. 'Why don't you kill me?' he whispered, dribbling. 'Why don't you kill me? I can't stand any more.'

'He's been saying that all morning, the dirty bastard,' was the sergeant's unfeeling comment.

But Montgomery was a professional soldier. He had seen much of horror and death in his time and was above resentment and revenge. Duly he reported the discovery of the infamous concentration camp to the War Office in London. Later he went to see the camp himself. Afterwards he wrote to one of his correspondents, 'The concentration camp at Belsen is only a few miles from my own present HQ. You have actually to see the camp to realize fully the things that went on: the photographs (enclosed) were all taken by a photographer from my HQ.' Sardonically he added, 'The SS Commandant is a nice looking specimen.'

Petty as he could be about his personal reputation, Montgomery lacked vindictiveness; unlike Eisenhower, who, after seeing his first concentration camp in Southern Germany, rounded on a somewhat bored-looking GI with, 'Now you know what we're fighting for,' Montgomery had no time for such recriminations. He was prepared to let lesser authorities deal with those responsible for perpetrating such atrocities. His concern was with fighting, and winning, the war.

This Sunday he had received his final orders for the rest of the campaign in Europe. Berlin was 'off' once again, but his own rôle had been upgraded from that of a mere flank guard to Bradley. Bradley's line on both sides of the Elbe had been relegated to a holding front, uselessly tying up nearly twenty US divisions. Montgomery, meanwhile, was, as we have seen, to seize the northern ports and 'be prepared to conduct operations to liberate Denmark', as well as 'clearing western Holland, north-eastern Holland and the coastal belt and enemy naval bases and fortification which threaten the approaches to Hamburg.'

It was a tall order for the Canadian 1st and the British 2nd Armies. Both were seriously short of riflemen and the War Office had already withdrawn one Canadian and one British division from Italy to help bolster them up. In the previous month's fighting the Canadians had lost 16,000 dead, of which over 10,000 were from British divisions fighting under Canadian command.

By now the British Army was more than a match for the Germans, after five long years of fighting, but the Germans still had the better weapons. Many of the British rank-and-file were in their teens, as indeed were the Germans opposing them, and the British battalion commanders in their late twenties, with brigadiers not much older. They were all expert in night fighting, infiltration and combat in woods, skills which up to now had been dominated by the Germans. Still, they were tired by constant action, with divisions such as the 43rd, 51st and 53rd depleted by severe losses. And in the fighting soon to come Montgomery knew that his prime need would be for the Poor Bloody Infantry.

So the Field Marshal brooded that Sunday night over his cup of hot milk and biscuits in the solitude of his looted caravan, which had once belonged to a fierce Italian general in the desert.* How was he to carry out all the assignments Eisenhower had given him with the scant forces at his disposal? Would anything be known in the end of his drive northwest when the Americans now monopolized the Allied propaganda machine which seemed to release only information which suited the US Top Brass? As his friend and confidante Colonel 'Simbo' Simpson had written to him recently from London, 'I had hoped that SHAEF had seen sense as regards plans. It really is frightful to think of all the lives being wasted to satisfy American public opinion. If the American public only knew the truth.'

Montgomery knew that they didn't, and they probably never would if the American generals, in particular Bradley, had their way. After the war they would probably close ranks and keep the reasons for Eisenhower's strategic failures to themselves. The American Public would be told that all had gone to plan right from the start; and because their generals had given them victory in the end they would be satisfied.

Montgomery looked at the silver pocket watch hanging at the

---

* Most of his possessions in the field were looted. But then the Field Marshal had lost nearly all his personal effects in the 1941 Portsmouth Blitz.

side of his narrow bunk. He finished the last of his milk. In a moment the tank of his guard platoon would rumble up to the door of his caravan to protect him in his remote headquarters in the corner of a German field. There was still talk of the German underground movement known as the Werewolves and his staff didn't want to be taken by surprise.

2

16 – 20 APRIL

I

A WOODEN SWORD WITH COURAGE PROTECTS HOME AND HEARTH BETTER THAN A CANNON

Bremen had been under enemy artillery fire since the morning of 10 April, 1945. At regular intervals during the day British 105mm cannon had bombarded the city from positions between Dreye and Delmenhorst, where the 'Highway Decorators' of the 51th Highland Division lay.

Directed by a light artillery spotter plane, the Allied guns had ranged in on selective targets which would cause the maximum publicity and the maximum nuisance value to the hard-pressed citizens of the beleaguered city. Churches, counting houses, even the remaining bridge across the River Weser, had all been hit.

The citizens of Bremen were not as 'red' as the citizens of Hamburg, but still they protested.* They called upon the city's Battle Commandant, General Becker, to surrender. Germany's cause, they argued, would not be served by continuing to hold out against the enemy. But Becker turned them down flat. He knew what his fate would be if he surrendered now. He'd either end up in a concentration camp or being choked to death by a

* Hamburg was notoriously communist. Even in 1944 there were strong underground communist cells in the city. It was one city that Hitler rarely visited before the war, on account of its left-wing leanings.

133

length of chicken wire, as had so many *Wehrmacht* generals before him.

Besides, he guessed that the artillery bombardments were intended only to weaken the citizens' resolve and persuade them to surrender, but he felt that by now the average *'Bremer'* should be inured to such bombardments.

Becker had a point. By April, 1945, nearly 4,000 people had been killed in air raids since June, 1940, of which there had been 170, which had destroyed 60 per cent of the city, forcing half the population to flee. In addition 22,000 *Bremer* had been killed in action.

The remaining 300,000 citizens had gone to ground. Many of them lived permanently in the squalid concrete bunkers which dotted the city. Before the war Air Marshal Goering had boasted that if an enemy aircraft ever crossed the frontiers of the Reich, he would call himself 'Meier', a supposedly Jewish name. It had been a great joke at the time. Everyone knew that Goering's *Luftwaffe* was invincible. All the same, he had hedged his bets. Everywhere in the big cities overhead bunkers, some eight storeys high, had been built to take in those people who had no shelters of their own to hide in if the enemy *did* happen to manage to bomb Germany. Others had taken permanently to their cellars, reinforced now by great wooden or steel beams, or created kinds of caves in the ruins.

On the surface public services still functioned perfectly, but the reality was different. There was water, gas and electricity admittedly, but they were strictly rationed and available only at certain times of the day. After a raid they seemed to disappear altogether and then the civilians had to rely on standpipes for water and the mobile columns of the German Red Cross and the National Socialist Women's Organizations who cooked food in army 'goulash cannon' among the ruins and distributed at least one hot meal a day to those without the means to do so themselves.

The citizens, for the most part, were war-weary and afraid of what was to come when the Allies finally reached the battered city. In the suburbs, through which the assault had to come, the locals tried to sever their contacts with the *landser*, even if they came from the Bremen area. In a secret conference attended by

134

Paul Wegener, the local *Gauleiter*, Colonel-General Blaskowitz, commander of Army Group H, and the soldier responsible for the defence of North Germany, Field Marshal Busch, it was stated that immediately German troops evacuated a position, or in some cases before, the locals hoisted white flags and began to help the enemy. More than once villagers had approached the enemy secretly and, in order to save their villages, had outlined the German defences. Wegener, who usually kept his opinions to himself, now said that, 'such traitors should be shot out of hand without trial.'

It was a sentiment with which Busch agreed. Back in 1942, in Russia, one of the officers on his staff had complained that they were shooting Russian prisoners just outside the head-quarters window. Busch had snorted, 'Then draw the fucking curtains.'

Official propaganda, while agreeing that the situation in Bremen was serious, tried to encourage the locals to believe in final victory. There was talk of new secret weapons which the Führer still had up his sleeve. Indeed there *was* such a weapon in Bremen that April. It was the new Walter U-boat Type XXI currently being built by the AG Weser company.* Others maintained that it wouldn't be long before the Anglo-Americans fell out with the advancing Russians and would soon be fighting on Germany's side against the 'Bolshevik hordes'.

In the end the official propagandists employed by Dr Goebbels simply appealed to the locals' sense of self-interest. What good would come of a British occupation, they asked. The notorious Morgenthau Plan would reduce Germany to the state of a slave economy. Germany's industrial might would be destroyed and the country would become one huge agricultural estate. What place would there be in such an economy for an industrialized, business-orientated Bremen? The citizens' livelihoods would vanish and all able-bodied men would be shipped to Russia or the once German-occupied countries to become

---

* Indeed, Ian Fleming had already formed his special 'Unit 39 Commando', one of whose task would be to capture the engine of this type of submarine before the Russians, the enemy of the future, got their hands on it. Fleming, the creator of 'James Bond', actually succeeded in doing this.

135

little better than slave labourers. As the local *Oldenburgische Staatszeitung* put it:

> *Ein Holzschwert mit Mut*
> *Schützt Hab und Gut*
> *Besser als eine Kanone – ohne**

Germans often complain about some other German that he or she lacks *'Zivilcourage'*, which can be roughly translated as 'lack of communal spirit', basically the inability to stand up to authority. Right from the start of the Second World War the aristocracy and the upper-class echelons of the *Wehrmacht* had plotted against Hitler, whom they held responsible for a war which would ruin Germany. But their efforts were half-hearted. Attack after attack on the Führer seemed to fail, not because Hitler took any special measures to ensure his personal safety, but because the plotters never seemed to get it right. Time after time their assassination attempts failed, almost as if they wished them to. When, in July, 1944, at the end of their tether and with defeat staring them in the face, the disaffected generals persuaded a brave young *Wehrmacht* colonel to sacrifice his own life to assassinate the Führer, the plotters made a hash of it. With all the resources available to them, (some suppose that even Field Marshal Rommel was privy to the plot) still couldn't get it right. That lack of *Zivilcourage* had let them – and the German people – down again.

Now, nine months after the failed 'July Assassination Plot', certain individuals in Bremen tried to assert the will of the majority who didn't want the city turned into a second Stalingrad by killing the representatives of the minority who wanted to continue the fight to the bitter end. These were the remaining top Nazis in Bremen and the senior Generals in North Germany, ranging from the soon-to-be 'second Führer' Grand Admiral Doenitz in Flensburg-Murwik, through Field Marshal Busch, down to the commander of the *Korps Ems*, General Siegfried Rasp.

---

* A wooden sword with courage, protects hearth and home, better than a cannon – without' (ie, without courage.)

These men, who had been young officers back in 1918 when the German Navy had mutinied against the defeated Kaiser and the Imperial Army had virtually disintegrated into a lawless left-wing mob, wanted no repetition of that disgraceful episode. Although he was to lose the Battle of Bremen, General Rasp was proud to point out to his interrogators afterwards that 'the German formations were tired, but nowhere did we encounter any instances of disobedience. The picture was totally different from that of 1917/18 at the end of World War One.' General Schaller, commander of the 8th Flak Division, which was to play an important rôle in the defence of Bremen, stated, when a PoW, that although after 1 May, when Hitler killed himself, 'Twenty men of my division deserted to the enemy, I had up to then no complaints about the mood and will to fight of my Division.'

It was, seemingly, a belief shared by many of the young soldiers who had come up through the ranks of the Hitler Youth and the Work Service (*Arbeitsdienst*). In that third week of April a 19-year-old officer in the 742 Light Infantry Regiment told his captors, when asked how soon it would take until the end of the war, 'When *we* win it. In the long term Germany will win this war. So long as one German lives he will fight against you . . . A race of masters, born to rule, cannot be turned into slaves.'*

Another soldier, trapped in mud up to his neck, told the British soldiers trying to drag him out, 'You think you've won. You've beaten us. But you're wrong. We'll still go on fighting till Germany wins.' It is not recorded if his captors then pulled him out!

Now a group of former Party officials, senior officers and ordinary citizens decided that the time had come to remove General Becker. The fear of the local Gestapo had diminished somewhat, for the members of the Secret State Police were making their own plans to find a fresh identity and take a 'dive' before the Allies arrived and placed them under 'automatic

* Looking at events in Europe fifty years later, one might feel that perhaps he was right.

arrest'.* Besides, some of the plotters who had finally discovered their *Zivilcourage* were policemen themselves. They would warn the conspirators in time if the Gestapo got on to their trail.

By now the plotters had got the measure of General Fritz Becker. The 55-year-old infantry general, who had twice successfully commanded an infantry division in the East and had won the Knight's Cross of the Iron Cross before being invalided back to the Reich and given the not so strenuous post of Battle Commandant of Bremen, was not an outstanding Nazi. Indeed it seems that he never joined the Party. But he *was* a German nationalist who would not betray his oath to the Führer as Commander-in-Chief of the Armed Forces. So there was only one way to get rid of him, as he was obviously not prepared to treat with the Allies, and that was to murder him.

Surprisingly enough the men who planned the assassination were those who would have normally been regarded as the pillars of the establishments: the head of the Bremen Police, Johannes Schroers, a man who by the nature of his post had to have been a Nazi, and the President of the local Chamber of Commerce, Dr Karl Bollmeyer.

Their first idea was to use local anti-fascist workers to do it for them. Even at this stage of the war there were still very few 'anti-fascists' prepared to take up arms against the Nazi Regime,** but in the shipyards which lined the Weser and were traditionally 'red', the plotters found 100 or so anti-fascist workers who were prepared to make an armed attack on Becker's HQ if Colonel Raspe, a member of Becker's staff known to be in sympathy with them, was prepared to help them. But Colonel Raspe obviously lacked *Zivilcourage* and declared that any

* Even before the Invasion Allied Intelligence had prepared black lists, right down to the lowest levels, of those Germans who would come under the 'automatic arrest' category once their area was captured by the Allies. This surprised not only the Germans concerned but also the Allied troops involved in the operation. Neither had thought that Allied Intelligence was that efficient.

** Later, when Bremen had already fallen, 10,000 anti-fascists were registered in the city, but by then there was no danger from the authorities and no need for *Zivilcourage*.

attack on Becker's bunker HQ was a *'Himmelfahrtskommando'* (an 'Ascension Day Command', a one-way attack from which there was no return).

An appeal was made to the workers' unofficial representative, the future head of Germany's largest postwar union, IG Metall, Willy Hundertmark, but he too turned them down. After the war Hundertmark, a prominent socialist and a member of the 'Association of those persecuted by the Nazi Regime', stated that, 'We had no weapons. Where were we supposed to get them from? A revolt would have meant certain death. After all there were still lots of Nazis and *they* had the weapons.'

In the end Schroers and Bollmeyer had to turn to, of all people, the local police. Forty or fifty of them, all heavily armed, were to arrest Bremen's top Nazis. As it was expected that General Becker would respond to the coup with force, the police were told to shoot him.

But at the very last moment the two leaders got cold feet and called off the mission. According to his own story, Bollmeyer decided that he personally would shoot Becker. He made arrangements to call at the house of his good friend *Direktor* Stapelfeldt of the ship-building firm AG Weser. It was at Stapelfeldt's villa at No.95 Parkallee that Becker had his lodgings. Bollmeyer rang the bell, pistol hidden in his pocket, and waited. A maid answered the door and said, *'Leider ist der Herr General nicht zu hause'* (Unfortunately the General is not at home). With that the would-be killer had to be content. He lived to continue his business in Bremen after the war as a respected and honoured businessman who had actually *fought* the Nazis, unlike most of his kind.

Zivilcourage had failed once again and General Becker lived on to fight the Battle of Bremen.

II

WE'D RATHER FUCK THAN FIGHT

General Becker now began to dispose his troops for a large-scale battle. He was faced by the same problem as that of his opponent, General Horrocks, Commander of the British XXX Corps – the front to be defended, and attacked, was simply too long for the resources available.

In Becker's case, for the defence of Greater Bremen he commanded some 8,000 men, half of them the hastily-called-up *Volkssturm*. They were poorly trained and poorly armed. They possessed no heavy weapons and relied mainly on automatics and panzerfaust bazookas, with which they were well equipped, as was the *Wehrmacht* at that time as a whole.

Along the line of the Weser he had three good formations, the 12th SS's Training and Reinforcement Battalion to his left flank and the 18th SS Training and Reinforcement Battalion to his right. Both numbered well over 1,000 eager Nazi troopers.

In between was the 2nd Marine Infantry Division, perhaps some 8,000 strong at this time. It was not so well trained as the SS, but its men were more mature, fitter and in their early twenties, and just as eager as the SS. On both flanks of Becker's long front were the four divisions of Rasp's *Korps Ems*, two infantry and two armoured. The latter were low on tanks, but both had excellent reputations, based on nearly four years of combat – the 'Great Germany Division', which was regarded as almost equivalent to an SS armoured division, and the 15th Panzergrenadier Division, which had gained a great fighting reputation in the Western Desert against the Eighth Army. In all these formations were outnumbered by about three to one by Horrocks' five divisions. But they were on the defensive and, whereas Horrocks intended to make a decisive breakthrough on this long front, with a major river and flooded land to guard it, he would need to be in overwhelming strength.

But where was Horrocks to attack, bearing in mind that once he had crossed the river and the floodlands, he would have to assault a major built-up area, ideal for defence? It was a problem that worried Becker too. He knew, of course, that the British wouldn't attempt a central assault. That would be too costly in casualties. Horrocks would launch his first assault from the flank. But which would it be? From the south-west where Becker's troops were thin on the ground, and he was relying on the flooded fields there to hold up the Tommies until they reached the defended suburbs? Or from the south-east where the enemy would have to capture the key road junction at Verden on the other side of the river line in order to drive on into the city?

General Horrocks decided that a feint was needed to fool the German defenders as to where the main thrust, the *Schwerpunkt* of his attack, would come and chose the south-west flank and the waterlogged fields, where in some cases boats would be needed, for this assault. To carry it out he called upon the oldest division in the British Army, which had gained the proud nickname of the 'Iron Division' for its steadfastness in the trenches in the First World War.

In 1939 the then General Montgomery took the 3rd Division to France to join the BEF. Came the débâcle and Montgomery, who had given the Third its distinctive triangle divisional sign, led it to safety from the fighting in Louvain to the beaches at Dunkirk. As a result of his leadership, the Third was really the only British division to reach the United Kingdom that summer with most of its weapons intact.

Surprisingly enough for a regular division, the Third did not go overseas, but trained, trained and trained again, until D-Day when it finally joined in the fray. By now the Third was a typical division of its time, its rank and file predominantly English, though by 1945 it did number the King's Own Scottish Borderers, the Ulster Rifles and some minor foreign formations among its ranks. Its battalions were not among the 'posh' ones favoured by moneyed young men, but recruited in places such as East Yorkshire, Lancashire and Norfolk.

They were solid, tough regiments which had battle honours dating back as long as the Division itself, and they did well what they were called upon to do in battle, as had their predecessors. Stolidly, the Third's infantry had plodded that long path across Europe from France into Belgium and from there to Holland and Germany. As far as is known there were no scandals associated with the Third, as with some other British infantry divisions. Its commander was not changed to put more 'pep' into a formation which was losing its drive. There were no battalions which refused to go into action or broke and fled in the face of severe resistance. The Third did the job that was expected of it, always securing its objectives regardless of casualties, and in France and Holland they were heavy. But naturally the handful of survivors still with the Third from D-Day were careful, slightly cynical young men, who had seen it all before, and then some. They knew when to move and they knew when to keep their heads down. If asked by foolish journalists what their aims were, more often than not these cheerful young men would reply, 'Well, we'd rather fuck than fight!'

Corporal Fred Pettinger of the 2nd Lincolns was one of the lucky ones. He had been in action since D-Day and by the law of averages he should have been wounded or killed by this time, but he hadn't. Ironically a German would put him in hospital for six weeks *after* the war, when a Nazi prisoner threw black pepper in his eyes and blinded him. The German didn't live to tell the tale.* Now, with what was left of his original platoon, Pettinger was going into action again.

The circumstances of the battle to come between the men of the Iron Division and the 1000-odd trainees of the newly constituted *Horst Wessel Division*, named after the pimp-martyr of the pre-1933 Nazi movement, but currently called *Kampfgruppe Hoblik*, after its CO, were exceptional. For both sides knew, whether they liked it or not, that the war was over. The Germans could fight only with blind fanaticism, hoping perhaps for some

* Fifty years on, 74-year-old Mr Pettinger still suffers periodic periods of near-blindness.

miracle from on high to save the day. As for the British, they had everything to gain by remaining alive for the next few days. Already the rank and file knew the demobilization date of their particular group and even the most dim-witted among them could work out to the week when they would be discharged.

But now they were expected to risk their lives against fanatical young SS men dug in in a largely built-up area and only too willing to die willingly for Folk, Fatherland and Führer. Ahead of them lay a full-scale divisional attack, mounted along the three main roads leading to Bremen, with two brigades, the 9th and the 185th, in the lead, and the 8th in reserve, once it had kicked off the initial attack.

The Suffolks led the way. The going at first was easy. There were few German troops dug in around the villages along the main road from Fahrenhorst to Brinkum and it was obvious to General 'Bolo' Whistler, the cheerful, seemingly always smiling commander of the Third, that the enemy was relying on the fact that British armour couldn't easily deploy in the waterlogged fields on either side of the road. All the same, he was a realist and experienced enough to know that the Germans would start defending the area once they had assessed the strength of the attack.

Prisoners taken by the Germans told them that an attack on Bremen was in the offing, a fact which was confirmed when German reconnaissance planes spotted some forty to fifty British tanks and bridging equipment waiting to move up. The German Intelligence Officers didn't need a crystal ball to know that that bridging equipment was intended for a crossing of the Ochtum and later the Weser.

The Third pushed on and were soon under shellfire from the villages of Gross Mackenstedt, Leeste and a farm at Erichshof. Still sticking to the road, because the engineers had so far been unable to check the fields for mines, the Suffolks and the South Lancs headed for the three villages from which the shelling was coming. Here, they now knew, were elements of the 18th SS waiting to stop them before they reached the key village of Brinkum.

The pace started to hot up as the leading troops were subjected to the feared 'moaning minnies' dropping 105mm shells in rows of six on them before the trucks bearing the electric mortars sped away to new firing positions. The 88mm cannon of the 8th Flak Division joined in. Again that old screeching sound, like a piece of canvas being ripped apart, flooded the sky. Great holes appeared to the advancing troops' front. But the men of the Iron Division were not deterred. They pushed on doggedly and caught a battery of the 8th Flak Division by surprise. With prods from their bayonets they forced the scared kids to turn their 88mms round. Thereupon the British infantry fired the remaining shells into the German positions. Soon thereafter the SS launched their first counter-attack. Although the Bremen newspapers proclaimed it a victory, in reality it was a defeat. The SS turned and ran. As one company commander commented, observing the fleeing SS, 'They say they want to die for their bloody Führer. Let's give 'em the honour of doing just that.' That day the second-in-command of the 18th SS, plus another eighty SS, surrendered to the Third.

But it wasn't all beer and skittles. The Iron Division was taking casualties too, at a time when they least wanted to be killed or wounded. Men who had survived the fighting all the way from the Beaches now died with victory in sight.

Major 'Banger' King of the 2nd East Yorkshires had become something of a mascot to the battalion. Dour, always sucking on his old pipe, fast approaching middle age, he had encouraged the troops heading for the shore on D-Day with readings from Shakespeare's *Henry V*. Perhaps it hadn't been their kind of literature. All the same over the months that followed his bravery and care for his men had become legendary, not only in the East Yorks, but throughout the whole division. As the divisional historian wrote after the war, 'The whole Division was proud of Major King and saw him as a representative of all that was best in themselves.'

But King was not fated to survive. Delivering rations to his forward company in Gross Mackensen, his carrier went over a mine. He died while being carried back. Another of the 'originals' had not made it.

III

. . . CLEARED UP THE SITUATION COMPLETELY, AND AS FAR AS I WAS CONCERNED, BREMEN WAS FINISHED

Corporal Pettinger was determined *he* would survive. He hadn't come this far to die with the end in sight.

The Lincolns, of the 9th Brigade, had now taken the lead on the road from Brinkum to Bremen with the King's Own Scottish Borderers on their right flank. As usual, their CO, Lieutenant-Colonel Cecil Firbank, was up front with them. Always ready to take part in any firefight as an ordinary rifleman, he was there waiting for whatever opportunity presented itself.

Pettinger's platoon advanced over the wet fields through the darkness. Somewhere 'Crocodiles' of the 7th Royal Tanks were at their deadly work, spraying German positions with bursts from their flamethrowers. To the infantry's front signal rockets were hissing into the sky above the enemy positions, but so far the SS had not become aware of the advancing Lincolns.

A lone German twin-engined bomber started to circle above the crossroads on the far side of Brinkum, but no one fired at it as they didn't want to give away their positions. Finally, as if in disgust, the German plane dropped three small bombs and went back the way it had come. One bomb killed a black and white Holstein cow. The platoon pressed on and still all remained comparatively quiet. But Pettinger and the other old sweats didn't trust the quietness. They knew the Jerries were up there

145

to their front somewhere in the darkness. At times when the wind blew in the right direction they were sure they could smell that peculiar German odour, a mixture of unwashed bodies, garlic and the coarse black tobacco which they smoked.

And then it happened. The young fanatics of the SS rose from their hiding places and charged, shouting their futile battle cry, *'Alles für Deutschland'*. In this case it wasn't very much. Simply a .303 British bullet, which all too often ended that battle cry for ever.

How long that battle in the half-darkness lasted Fred Pettinger never could remember. But when it was over he discovered that his platoon had lost three dead and four wounded. Bad enough at this stage of the war, but nothing compared with the total losses of the 18th SS that night. At a cost of twenty dead, thirty wounded and several missing in the two brigades of the Third, sixty German soldiers and eleven civilians were killed, plus 300–400 SS men taken prisoner. That night the 18th SS lost half its strength.

That morning the German command in Bremen took stock of the situation after the attack from the south-east. Already the *Kreisleiter* (Nazi County Leader) responsible for the general Brinkum area had reported to Becker and the Party officials that the whole area south of Brinkum and Gross Mackenstedt was in enemy hands and a full-scale attack on Bremen itself was expected any day now. However, the *Kreisleiter* had one reservation. In common with most civilians, while he expected the main assault to come in from that general area, it wouldn't come from the south-west but from the south. His reasoning was that, although the main British attack had started in the British Third Division's area, to their left flank, ie. to the south, there was the 51st Highland Division, plus the 2nd Canadian Division, and possibly the Polish Armoured Division, all of which were currently underemployed. Weren't they in reserve waiting to make the decisive attack on Bremen when the line of the Weser had been breached?

We do not know General Becker's reaction to this, nor that of *Gauleiter* Wegener. All we do know is that neither of them made any attempt to shift any troops to meet such a threat. So the defences were left as they were, with the key town of

Verden being covered solely by the 2nd Marine Division and what was left of the 12th SS. It was a recipe for disaster.

On that same 17 April when General Becker decided that no change in his defences was needed, although he still remained puzzled as to the Tommies' intentions, General Horrocks was equally at sea.

'Jorrocks' as he was known to his men, didn't like the idea of tackling the built-up area of the city one bit. At this stage of the war he didn't want to waste more lives than necessary or inflict more misery on the German civilians, whom, he knew, the British would soon have in their Zone of Occupation. He was in a quandary as to where he should attack successfully and with the fewest possible casualties.

For a while he had tried to convince his neighbouring corps commander, General Ritchie, who led XII Corps, currently engaged in the Hamburg – River Elbe area, to take over Bremen. But Richie wasn't having it. He turned the 'kind offer' down, indicating that his Corps had advanced too far now to turn back and deal with Bremen. Miserably, Horrocks looked at the problem facing him anew.

It was now that Montgomery turned up at the newly captured village of Leeste in the Third Division's area. Outside one of the typical red-brick farmhouses of the area he conferred with Horrocks in his map lorry.*

Montgomery was in a strange mood. Perhaps it was due to the dithering over Berlin and the total change of plan which now made him responsible, with a SHAEF priority from Eisenhower himself, for capturing Bremen and North Germany. Perhaps it was personal: the realization that he personally appeared not to be in the running for the kudos of final victory, and that once the war was ended his personal prestige and power would vanish.

Thus he appeared in the April sunshine, dressed in sloppy civilian trousers and a shabby oilskin jacket, through which a pullover he had worn that winter still showed, and proceeded to

---

* Horrocks, like Montgomery, was not fond of large HQs. He preferred small informal CPs. Once, during the battle of the Rhineland, he was spotted up a tree directing a battle. In Bremen he did so one day from the upper floor of a semi-detached house.

brief his Corps Commander by means of a large-scale map he had brought with him.

It wasn't customary in the British Army for army commanders to tell somebody like Horrocks, who led 100,000 men, how to fight his next battle. But Horrocks didn't resent the interference. By this time he had acquired total confidence in the 'master'. Horrocks felt, too, that he had made a couple of bad mistakes in the long campaign, including the mess at Antwerp when he had failed to clear the estuary leading to the port, and his tardiness at Arnhem which had meant the destruction of the First Airborne Division. On both occasions Montgomery had let him make his own decisions and, although he had failed, had not sacked him, though throughout the campaign Montgomery had been ruthless with other commanders he had felt had not come up to his high standards.

Montgomery's visit had caught Horrocks almost by surprise. Army group commanders didn't usually appear some five miles behind the fighting front, guarded by a solitary armoured car, with the thunder of the guns on the firing line quite audible. All he knew was from a quick telephone call from one of Monty's staff officers that the Army Commander was on his way. Now here he was, ready to get down to the business of what to do with Bremen.

Monty wasted no time, 'Jorrocks,' he said, 'I am *not* happy about Bremen.'

'Nor am I, sir,' Horrocks replied, glad that the point had been brought into the open from the start.

'Tell me about it,' Montgomery said, sitting down and looking at the map. He listened while Horrocks pointed out the difficulties of attacking a large area of shattered buildings which would make an ideal defensive position.

He pondered over the matter for a few minutes, as if he were considering Horrocks' problems in the light of what he already knew, before stabbing the map with his forefinger and snapping, 'We will do A . . . B . . . C . . . and D.' There was no subsequent discussion. He simply took four decisions, which, as Horrocks wrote after the war, 'cleared up the situation completely, and as far as I was concerned Bremen was finished.'

Thereupon Montgomery got on to the bonnet of a jeep outside

the farmhouse and, hands behind his back, head raised and slightly tilted, addressed the troops for the benefit of the army photographers and the troops themselves, who one day could boast to their grandchildren that once 'Field Marshal Montgomery talked to us just before we captured Bremen.' Then he was off, as swiftly as he had arrived.

As Horrocks wrote 'From his point of view Bremen was finished and, as I knew very well, he would now relegate it to the back of his mind, while he went on to consider the next problem.

But Horrocks knew nothing of what was going on in the C-in-C's mind that day. It was the Yanks again. So far they had hardly noticed his campaign in the north. Even after Eisenhower had made the capture of Bremen one of his main priorities, the Supreme Commander had made no attempt to visit Montgomery. He had indeed visited his generals carrying out their purposeless campaign in the south, had been appalled by what he had seen in Buchenwald and angered by Patton's remark after viewing the German gold reserves hidden in a former mine at Merkers that he, Eisenhower, and Bradley should keep the hoard secret and 'take a little bit out each year' to pay their soldiers and buy new weapons, 'so they'd be ready for the Russian attack.' But he hadn't visited Montgomery, once more commanding well over a million of his men.

In the meantime there was constant criticism coming from those same Americans who at the beginning of the month had relegated his armies to the rôle of a flank guard, that Montgomery was not moving fast enough. Why hadn't he crossed the Elbe? If the Russians beat him there, Eisenhower felt, there'd be all hell to pay. There were already American troops on the west side and if they had to fall back in favour of the Russians, they would be committing the unpardonable sin of giving up territory bought with American lives.

Eisenhower, Montgomery already knew, had appealed to the Chief of the Imperial General Staff, Alan Brooke, and told him, as we have seen, that he had done everything in his power to get Montgomery moving. He had concluded the cable referred to earlier by telling Brooke that he had formed a reserve for

Montgomery's use and that, in effect, he now washed his hands of 'responsibility for any further delay.'

Bradley agreed with his boss that Montgomery needed a push. 'I expressed strong doubt that Monty could carry out his Lübeck mission without our virtually forcing US troops on him,' he wrote later. He opined, too, that the commander of the troops in question, General Ridgway, who led the XVIII Airborne Corps, would make Monty move. 'No one can build a fire under Monty better than Ridgway.' As Bradley wrote maliciously in his memoirs: 'Had we not primed Ridgway in advance and then rushed him to help Monty, the Russians would surely have reached the Danish border first and perhaps gone on to Copenhagen with possibly damaging consequences in the postwar world.'

In the end, when they came to write their memoirs after the war, in a changed climate of opinion when Russia was the new enemy, these generals who had been so concerned that April with the capture of prestige targets of no political importance in Southern Germany made it seem that Montgomery was the one who lacked geo-political foresight. They had pressed for action in the north while Monty had sat on his thumbs and done nothing. As Montgomery remarked, now that the Americans were urging him to move before the Russians got to the Baltic, 'This is adding insult to injury.'

IV

THE OLD TIN OF BULLY BEEF OR A PACKET OF FAGS OPENED ALL DOORS. THEY WERE THE SIGN OF REALLY TRUE LOVE

The advancing British were caught completely off guard. The men of the Ox & Bucks, the Highland Light Infantry and what was left of the 1/5th Welch had felt they had finished off the 2nd Marine Division in the three battles for Rethem. Now, led by the 53rd Division's Reconnaissance Regiment, fanning out in the heathland on the other side of the River Aller, the leading infantry thought they were in complete charge of the situation. Admittedly Intelligence had warned them that Marines, supported by the remainder of the German 480th Division, were forming up in Verden, which was their objective. But the infantry were not unduly worried. They felt that the heart had gone out of the defenders of the river line and it would only be a matter of days before they gave up altogether. After all, German prisoners had been surrendering to them ever since they had crossed the river and begun their north-westerly advance. Now it was their turn to repeat that time-honoured formula that so many British soldiers had heard, with the familiar sinking feeling, over the last few years, 'For you the war is over.'

The Ox and Bucks, leading the 71st Brigade, had been hitting German strongpoints hidden in the trees either side of the road from Gross Hauslingen. Their casualties hadn't been high, but as always it had been the best men who were killed, the ones the Division could least afford, the subalterns and senior NCOs. But the prisoners kept coming and the Brigade was still moving.

Then the Germans launched a surprise attack. They advanced shoulder to shoulder in a kind of massed bayonet charge which the young infantrymen remembered from the Hollywood movies of trench warfare in the First World War, and they were actually singing.

As Private Desmond Milligan of the Oxs and Bucks recalled, 'They attacked our two companies in a massed wave reminiscent of World War One. They charged shoulder to shoulder, singing their war songs and shouting encouragement to each other!'

It was no different in the area of The Highland Light Infantry. They were hit at one in the morning. As Captain Pender recalled, 'It happened after two companies had done a long three-mile outflanking movement across country. The two Company Commanders and myself were standing on the road prior to taking up defensive positions when we heard marching feet approaching from the east. Major Hemilryke, OC 'B' Coy, hailed them, thinking it was 'C' or 'D' Coy. Immediately heavy firing broke upon us. Major H was severely wounded and a number of Jocks were killed or wounded along the track to our left rear. Things became particularly unpleasant.'

The Marines might well have been drugged or drunk, or both. It was customary in German formations, if schnapps was not available, to supply the attackers with 'chococola', a thick rich chocolate bar mixed with what used to be called 'benzies'. Not only did the drug keep the soldiers awake far beyond the normal period, but it put them on a 'high' in which they were beyond caring about being shot or killed. Now, bellowing the *Horst Wessellied*, they slammed into the Highland Light Infantry. The Jocks did their best, but they had been caught by surprise after a long and exhausting day. The Marines started to push them back and both sides were taking casualties, but the Jocks were getting the worst of it and started to go to ground in the drainage ditches at the sides of the road.

Pender, who had now taken over 'B' Company, and Major Greenway of 'A' tried their best to withdraw the trapped Jocks to stand and fight in a better position. As Pender recalled, 'It was difficult in the dark to find my Company. Some were in a flooded ditch, some under a bridge, some in a scrub plantation.' He did his best, whistling up the stretcher-bearers to carry away the wounded, but he didn't want to waste too much time in this untenable position. So it was with a heavy heart that he ordered the stretcher-bearers not to try and retrieve those Jocks who had fallen inside the enemy positions. It was heartrending to hear their cries and pleas as they realized that they were being abandoned, but Pender knew that there was no alternative.

Now he started to pull the Jocks back. 'All the time the Germans were bringing fire to bear on the track. I pulled some of the Jocks physically as I could not make myself heard. Eventually everyone who was on his feet got back to 'A' Company. A pretty sorry-looking lot we were too. Some had lost their weapons and both Companies' 18 sets were broken.'

Still the young German fanatics applied the pressure and still the Jocks fought back, with those who had no weapons taking over those of their comrades who were hit. In the darkness the Germans could come very close to the rough-and-ready 'scrapes' which were all the protection that the Jocks had been able to dig for themselves. Everyone prayed for an air strike, but the darkness prevented that and, besides, their radios with which they might have called up a 'cab rank'* to help them were both off the air.

Just after dawn there was a lull in the fighting and a one-hour truce was arranged – the German Marines invariably turned out to be fair fighters – to retrieve the wounded on both sides. A young British officer, Lieutenant Jim Hillier, went out to meet the Germans and somehow got into conversation with a German officer who spoke English. The latter said, 'I shall like to shake hands with an honourable Englishman.' Hillier corrected him, '*Scotsman*,' he said, though in fact he was one of those many Englishmen who served with Scottish regiments during the war and became more of a Scot than the native articles. He added, 'You speak very good English.' The German enlightened him,

---

* A standing patrol of fighter-bombers which hovered over the battle waiting for a call for action.

'Yes, I was at Oxford University,' then added hurriedly, 'Firing will start in five minutes' time.'

It did. Again a mess of confused fighting was the result, with an HLI Bren gun unfortunately shooting up a German ambulance filled with wounded Marines by mistake. But it was a measure of the respect that the Jocks showed for these German Marines that a stretcher-bearer, Private Buller, stayed with the wounded Germans until they were picked up.

And so it went on. All day long the Jocks were under constant fire. It was too dangerous on that flat, wet plain to evacuate the wounded and so they stayed there and died with the rest, including Major Hemilryke who had been wounded at the outset of the attack. So they waited, and fought, and prayed, and ran out of compo rations, with only ditch water to sustain them until in the distance they heard the rumble of the tanks coming to relieve them.

But, hard-done-to as they were, they were still the Jocks of the 1st Battalion, the Highland Light Infantry, hard men belonging to a proud regiment. As the tanks breasted the rise and the equally weary Germans started to pull back, the surviving NCOs got up from their holes and scrapes crying, 'All right there. Let's be having yer. Bags o' swank now.' They were the age-old cries of the British Army in which, even now, bullshit reigned supreme. Mud-splattered, hungry and weary, but with arms at the slope, the survivors returned to Battalion HQ with the company pipers playing them back.

Still the advance went on. Bobby Ross, cheerful commander of the 53rd Division to which the attacking infantry belonged, was putting on the pressure now. His tactics were somewhat wooden and old-fashioned, but perhaps he was under too much pressure from above. All the same the casualties were mounting steadily, with his 158th and 160th Brigades, 'played out', according to Colonel Crozier, commanding the Division's Manchester machine-gun battalion, and all the troops, according to the same source, 'very tired'.

Roughly at the same time as the 3rd Division at the other end of the Bremen front was concluding its feint, the men of the 53rd were on the high ground overlooking their objective, Verden, preparing to attack. By now the Germans had brought up new troops and it looked as if Becker was prepared to make a fight for the city. Ross, no longer his usual cheerful self, didn't like that one bit. One of the three battalions of the 158th Brigade, the 1/5th Welch, had suffered heavy casualties at Rethem and the other two, the 7th Royal Welch Fusiliers and the 1st East Lancs, were full of reinforcements – the Division had absorbed 4,000 only three weeks before – and he wondered if they could carry out their assignment against fresh German troops who were well dug in. Still there was nothing for it. The high ground had to be won before Verden could be taken. Colonel Tyler, CO of the 7th RWF, was ordered to attack.

At midday the Typhoons fell out of the sky, cannon pounding away. 20mm shells streamed towards the German artillery position. Time and again the 'Tiffies' went on against the defenceless Germans. Slowly but surely the high ground was transformed into a lunar landscape, with great holes every-where, woods burning and shattered farmhouses billowing smoke. An hour later the Welch were up on the heights only to find them abandoned.

Their comrades of the East Lancs, ordered to capture the nearby village of Kirchlinteln, were not so lucky. All tracks leading to the houses huddled around the little church were covered by dug-in German machine guns and the troops there were prepared to give a good account of themselves. They wouldn't break and run.

H-hour came and the British 25-pounders opened fire with a tremendous roar, Shells poured down on Kirchlinteln, which the attacking soldiers had been told was a hospital town and might well be soon abandoned. But it wasn't. When the barrage finally lifted and the British infantry prepared to charge the German defenders were waiting for them.

'A' Company, the 1st East Lancs, took the brunt of the first volleys. Mortars whined and sent their bombs winging towards the attackers. Spandaus opened up and then all was confusion and sudden death. The company commander, Major White-side, and most of his platoon leaders were wounded. Tanks supporting the attack were knocked out at close range by Germans with panzerfausts. More and more East Lancs fell. Desperately, Colonel Allen, their CO, combined his badly hit 'A' and 'B' companies. They attacked the village itself. The savage mêlée swayed back and forth, with the first German prisoners, drafted from the *Luftwaffe*, complaining that they had been rushed into action so swiftly that they didn't even know to which formation they belonged. 'Crocodile' tanks joined in the fight. Dodging the panzerfaust rockets time and again, they waddled up and down the village street squirting their deadly flames, at any sign of resistance. Slowly but surely the Germans' will to resist started to weaken, especially when they saw the flame-throwing tanks. More and more came out of their machine-gun nests and strongpoints begging for mercy.

Finally all fight seemed to drain from the defenders of Verden. The men of the Ox and Bucks found the going surprisingly easy for once. The Germans had promised to fight to the end to defend Verden, but that wasn't to be. Opposite the cemetery the Ox and Bucks attacked a small housing estate. It was a virtual walkover. One German defender was killed and 112 surrendered. The only resistance seemed to come from the womenfolk, as Private Milligan recorded: 'We flushed out some young Germans hiding in a shed. Their weapons were lying all over the place. Their womenfolk thought we were going to shoot them and pleaded for their lives. Nazi propaganda had done its work well.' But the young soldiers lived to become old men and die in their beds.

So they moved into Verden. By evening the town at the southern end of the Bremen front was securely in British hands. German propaganda had maintained that their 'brave soldiers and *Volkssturm*' would fight to the bitter end. Instead the defenders had slipped away into the night leaving the inhabitants to drape their houses with anything white to show that for them at least the war was over.

But the advance guard was on the lookout for any treachery, despite the relief that they wouldn't have to fight for this built-up area. They need not have worried. The locals were more scared of them than they were of the Germans. As one of the soldiers described it at the time, 'The German civilians gazed in horror. We did look awesome. We were encrusted with dust and grime and heavily armed and had 48 hours of beard. Hitler's propaganda had told them we would rape and loot and kill all before us.'

But as another Oxs and Bucks soldier said, 'We were just too bloody knackered even for the raping bit. Then, when we'd recovered, the old tin of bully beef or a packet of fags opened all doors. They were the sign of really true love.'

3

20 – 27 APRIL

I

EVERYTHING PASSES.
AFTER EVERY DECEMBER
THERE IS ALWAYS A MAY

Now Bremen waited. The citizens knew that the start of the tragedy to come wasn't far off. Since the Tommies had advanced to the Weser the artillery bombardment of the city had increased tenfold. Party officials had been receiving details of casualties from all the suburbs – Arsten, Oberholz, Vahrer Strasse, the station area – for forty-eight hours now. They knew what that widespread bombardment signified. The Tommies were grouping for an all-out attack somewhere along the line, but they were trying to fool the defenders where it would take place by this widespread artillery bombardment.

The citizens stuck to the safety of their shelters whenever possible. Those who had reserves of food started to eat them up. What good would reserves be when they were dead?

When they were forced out of their shelters to fetch water or the pathetic bread ration they wore their best clothes. They would need them no longer. There'd be no more christenings, weddings, parties – only funerals. *

Perhaps sensing the defeatist mood of the citizens, Becker spoke to them for the last time. He didn't use the normal radio channels – they were no longer available. Instead he used the *Drahtfunk* – the wireless link used to warn the inhabitants of

---

* Those of us who were there at the end were surprised by just how well dressed the locals were.

161

advancing enemy bombers in the past. He spoke in the harsh, clipped accents of a Prussian soldier, though in reality he was a pastor's son: 'The defence of the city must be conducted without any thought to the general situation. I say further to you that Bremen is faced with a difficult time to come. But we must stick together in the days to come.' No one liked the tone of his speech. But it didn't matter now. Nothing mattered now.

The Party, under the leadership of *Gauleiter* Wegener, sent the routine birthday telegram to the Führer trapped in Berlin. 'Despite everything,' the Party bosses proclaimed, 'we shall triumph in the end. May God, *mein Führer* give you strength and health to keep the German people alive and ensure their future.' Thereupon Martin Bormann, the Führer's grey eminence, promised Wegener seven new divisions to bolster up the 'Weser Front'. They never arrived of course. There weren't seven new *battalions* in the whole of northern Germany, let alone divisions.

On that day negotiations took place between the locals and the British at the villages of Etelsen and Baden on the matter of surrender. They were secret and what took place there has never been recorded. But whatever the terms were, they weren't acceptable to the Germans. Nothing more came of the secret meetings and the dawn-to-dusk bombardment of the city continued. In their cellars those who still owned gramophones played the same old record of the popular tune of that year over and over again. Its title was '*Ja geht alles vorüber. Es geht alles vorbei. Nach jedem Dezember, gibt's wieder ein Mai.*'

Then, between six and six thirty that evening, the British gunners opened fire from the village of Huchting, newly captured by the Iron Division. By the sound the shells made the *Bremer* could tell that these were something different. Were they using gas? The first of the shells from the Third Division's positions exploded with a soft muffled plop unlike the sharp harsh crack of high explosive. Instead of the singing noise of shrapnel scything through the air, there was the flutter of paper flying on all sides. The Tommies were firing leaflets.

It took some time for the *Bremer* to pick up the first printed message from Horrocks. Normally it was a punishable offence to collect them. After air raids Hitler Youth, under the strict supervision of their leaders and with firm orders not to read the enemy propaganda, were sent out to collect them before the civilians could do so. But the Hitler Youth had disappeared. They were manning the city's guns or serving in the *Volkssturm*. So, cautiously, taking care that they were not spotted by the Party's spies, the civilians picked them up and fled to somewhere where they could read them in safety.

Under the headline 'YOU HAVE THE CHOICE' they read: You have the choice of two alternatives: capture with the use of army and air force, or unconditional surrender. If the citizens agreed to the latter then they should send out those prepared to negotiate under the protection of a white flag. The leaflet ended with the grim warning, underlined in black: 'WE GIVE YOU 24 HOURS TO DECIDE'.

The news spread through the ruined city like wildfire. The terms of the British leaflet were discussed, not just by ordinary citizens but by the Party bosses and the City Administration. The local head of Civil Defence, Dr Fischer, called the powerful *Gauleiter* of Hamburg, Karl Kaufmann, and asked him to intervene with Field Marshal Busch. *Gauleiter* Wegener again got in touch with the most powerful man in Germany after Hitler, Martin Bormann. But he had plans of his own for what was left of the Reich. As for Becker, he always maintained afterwards, when the damage had been done, that, 'I never saw any of them. Nor did I know anything about their contents.' But that was afterwards.

In fact General Becker, the only man who could have saved Bremen that week, though it might have cost him his life to do so, *did* know about the leaflet – not from the British, but from the city's officials, up and including the top Nazi *Gauleiter*. That Saturday, after the *Prominenz* had half-decided to surrender to Horrocks, they took their case to Becker at his CP.

He seemed quite cheerful, even when they told him that if he didn't surrender the Tommies intended to bomb Bremen into submission – and by now all of them had experienced the ruthless air raids launched by Air Marshal Harris of the RAF. The General remained sanguine. He advised the civilians to 'keep their ears stiff' (*die Ohren steif halten*), as the German phrase has it, to keep up their spirits. Angered, Wegener snapped that Becker had just 'passed a sentence of death' on the city. But Becker wasn't impressed.

Now Wegener was in a quandary. Becker wouldn't surrender. The Admiral in charge of the docks had just told him he was going to mine them to prevent the Allies from using them. What was he to do? Again a senior German official who might have turned the scales if he had spoken out failed to do so. He lacked the necessary *Zivilcourage*. Instead, on the afternoon of Saturday, 21 April, 1945, he went on the 'radio wire' and told his anxious audience that the 'Allied ultimatum' was a 'trick, pure and simple'. After all, the leaflet wasn't signed by anyone in authority. There was still hope for Germany and Bremen if the local citizens kept their nerve and held on.

Wegener went on to depict the atrocities the Allies would commit if Bremen surrendered. For his part, if it came to a battle for the city, his listeners would not be disappointed in him. He personally would 'fight to the last'.

The next day Paul Wegener, the last *Gauleiter* of Bremen, disappeared back to his native city of Oldenburg. He was never seen again in Bremen.

Now, in the twenty-four hours that must pass until the ultimatum ran out and the bombing began, the citizens did strange, uncharacteristic things. They knew they had been abandoned by the Führer, the Party and the Army. It was up to each and every individual to make his own decisions now.

Police Sergeant Dietrich Roeper decided he'd undertake a daring one-man mission to the Tommies to sue for peace. First he set off for the Weser Bridge in the suburb of Uesen. Risking his neck in the front line, he stole a boat and crossed under the very eyes of the German Army garrison of the wrecked bridge. Somehow or other, on the far bank, he found civilian clothes. Then, crossing the fields and dodging patrols of both sides all the time by a hair's breadth, he made his way to a British divisional headquarters at the village of Langwedel. There he surrendered to the senior divisional Intelligence Officer.

It took hours for the humble police sergeant to convince the British that he was genuine. But in the end he convinced them that he had contacts with prominent citizens, police officers and those of the Army who wished to surrender. If the British didn't go ahead with the planned bombing, he promised, these people could be talked into giving up the city without a fight. According to him, the British finally agreed. They said it was too late to cancel the RAF attack on Bremen's electricity works and harbour facilities, but from then onwards they would attack only main centres of resistance. Thus the order to attack with 1,200 heavy bombers and 145 artillery batteries was cancelled and the town saved from further destruction.

On that day when people from all over Bremen, living in a kind of limbo, made their own decisions what should be done, another pillar of local society who had once supported the Nazi cause plucked up the courage to do what he thought was right, although it might have cost him his life. Shipowner Friedrich Ziebell learned that Saturday afternoon that his fleet of sixty ships which plied Germany's waterways were going to be blown up on 22 April as part of the Führer's scorched earth policy. With all the dockers and tugs he could find, he towed his fleet away to remote areas of the Weser where they survived the war. Then he took a 'dive' and waited for the British to come.

State prosecutor Dr Waldemar Seidel, soon to be arrested by the Americans as a confirmed Nazi, abandoned his office, ordered that every employee should be handed three bottles of wine from Bremen's *Ratskeller* and went home to fry the last of his potatoes in castor oil given to him by his local chemist. Helmut Reuther and Marga Schierloh attended the last Nazi marriage ceremony performed at Bremen's *Haus des Reichs* (politely they turned down the free copy of *Mein Kampf* offered to all newly married couples in favour of a cookery book), then they celebrated with black market roast rabbit and *Mokkatorte* before turning in at their local bunker to celebrate their honeymoon night – with two or three hundred other citizens!

Others simply played cards, ate the rest of their food, got drunk, or said their prayers. But not many. Praying had been out of favour for the last twelve years. Now it was too late.

II

BAGS O' SWANK . . . REMEMBER WHO YOU ARE

While the citizens of Bremen waited for what was to come, the British Army moved. Everywhere to the rear, the villages, the fields, the farms were packed with the 100,000 soldiers of Horrocks' XXX Corps. Around them were the White halftracks, Bedford three-tonner trucks, Churchill and Sherman tanks, 50-foot-long pontoon tractors – the great mass of death-dealing machinery, adorned with the white star of the British Liberation Army. And all were pointing one way – north to Bremen.

While their battalion commanders surveyed the waterlogged battlefield to come, the soldiers moved after dark in their thousands, filling the night air with the hum of their motors, clogging the road, tracks and fields.

There were five divisions in all. There were the 'Highway Decorators' of the 51st Highland on the Corps' extreme left flank. They wouldn't attack Bremen itself. They would make a feint for Delmenhorst and then on towards Bremervoerde – that is if *Korps Ems* would let them. Next to them was the Iron Division, the Third, which would kick off Horrocks' attack on Bremen. Horrocks and Montgomery were sure they would carry their objectives. Moving eastwards, the next division in the line was the 52nd Scottish Division, the biggest in the British Army at that time. For nearly four years it had been kept in Scotland, training as the Army's sole mountain division, for employment in Norway. Instead it had landed in the flattest part of Europe – the Walcheren Islands – in October, 1944. The 52nd was reckoned by Horrocks to be his best division because it still contained the highest percentage of well-trained leaders. Waiting in the wings behind the 52nd was Thomas's 43rd Wessex, very experienced but much battered, as we have seen. Then to the extreme right flank there was the Guards' Armoured Division with its divisional single-eye patch.

On the whole these troops were well behaved, save perhaps for Horrocks' Scottish infantry brought up in the depressed thirties with the gang fights of Edinburgh and Glasgow, though they weren't regarded as particularly aggressive by the Germans. At Arnhem SS General Bittrich, the one-legged commander of the SS Panzer Corps which defeated the 1st British Airborne Division, told his staff, 'We must remember that British soldiers do not act on their own initiative when they are fighting in a town, when it becomes difficult for officers to exercise control. They are amazing in defence, but we need not be afraid of their capabilities in attack.'

In a way he was right. By nature the 'squaddie', on average, moved slowly and at a deliberate pace, taking his cue from his officers, and it seems that the British Army lost more junior officers and senior NCOs in combat than other armies because the latter were the ones who kept the rank and file going. In many ways it was due to the class system which pervaded the British Army, as exemplified by the Guards' tradition of an ordinary soldier asking his officer, 'Permission to speak, sir?' before doing so.

But at the same time the British soldier seemed more inclined to accept adversity, poor conditions, poor food, poor pay, even poor weapons when compared with the German ones, than soldiers of other armies. He was a simple soul, his officers thought, content as long as he got his char, his fried bully and his free rations of fags.

But there was more to the average squaddie than that. The Army had plucked him from this humdrum civilian life of pub, pictures and palais de danse. He had learned to 'swing them arms, Bags o' swank, Remember who yer bleedin' are', the hoarse threats bellowed at him across windswept parade grounds by frightening sergeant majors and drill sergeants. During the Wednesday afternoons 'make do and mend', sitting to attention on his bunk, darning thick grey socks or sewing

167

buttons on collarless shirts, corporals had lectured to him on 'the traditions of the regiment'; while earnest, pink-faced subalterns, whose father and grandfathers and theirs before them had served in the Regiment, had also tried to instil the values of the 'Regiment' into them.

Suddenly they weren't simply 'Smith 175', another 'body', cannon fodder for some unknown battle to come. Now they had been transformed into a member of 'Pontius Pilate's Bodyguard', the oldest regiment in the British Army, so old that they had been the Roman governor of Palestine's bodyguard in Jesus's day; they had become the 'Buffs', 'the Diehards', 'Hell's Last Issue', 'the Shiny Seventh' and all the rest of those military nicknames, which meant nothing to the outside world from which they were now cut off, but very much to them.

Another dimension had been added to their lives, not just for the years of war, but for the rest of their times. Even when they were old men, those who survived, they would always remember the 'lads' and the 'old mob' and feel pride in what they had done once when they had been young and 'full of piss and vinegar'. Now for the last time in the Second World War, although they didn't know it then, perhaps for the last time in history a major British Army moved forward into battle with the slow, steady purpose of the British soldier.

Some were already in battle. On both flanks of Horrocks' corps the situation was fluid and uncertain. On Saturday, 21 April, while Bremen waited for 'bomber' Harris to send his dreaded visitors, the 51st Highland Division was probing forward on Horrocks' left flank against Rasp's *Korps Ems*, trying to discover the Germans' dispositions and intentions.

On the right flank the Guards Armoured Division was already engaged against the 15th Panzergrenadier Division, once the 15th Light Division of Rommel's Afrika Korps. The panzergrenadiers had been about to attack through the gap on the right which separated Horrocks from Ritchie's corps, when the Guardsmen hit them. This was the battle that would see the last Victoria Cross of the War in Europe.

Eddie Charlton, the 18-year-old son of a Manchester butcher, had volunteered for the Guards immediately the war broke out. His reasons had been both pragmatic and patriotic. At that time the Manchester Police Force only accepted probationary constables who had been guardsmen and Eddie Charlton dearly wanted to become a policeman. He also wanted to fight for his country. Instead he fought the authorities until 1940 when he was allowed to join the regiment of his choice, the Irish Guards, on the strength of some Irish connection rooted in the dim past.

A few months after D-Day he was finally posted to a fighting battalion in the Guards Armoured Division, commanded by General Adair, who had lost his own son killed in action in Italy. He joined a 300-year-old formation which seemed one of the last bastions of real privilege in 1945 in a British Army which would vote overwhelmingly for Labour in the first postwar election. In one battalion of the Division alone, the 3rd Scots Guards, there were, for instance, a future Archbishop of Canterbury, Lord Chamberlain, Home Secretary, Chief Scout, chairman of Rolls Royce and Senior Steward of the Jockey Club. But that didn't concern Guardsman Charlton. Now he was a Sherman tank driver with the Irish Guards' Number One Squadron commanded by Major O'Cock. After five years he was going into action at last.

That Saturday the Irish Guards' Number One Squadron probed towards Zeven, north-east of Bremen, in an attempt to cut the road between the city and Rotenburg. They had spotted a German convoy and had waited until the unsuspecting Germans rolled straight into the ambush they had set. At point-blank range the Micks opened up. The Germans hadn't a chance. The trucks slithered and skidded to a stop, with dead Marines of the 2nd Marine Infantry Division scattered on the road and forty of their trucks destroyed or captured.

Now the Irish Major, with the name which had caused him a lot of grief in his youth, ordered four Shermans under Lieutenant Quinan, in whose tank Charlton rode, to leave the rest and head for the village of Wistedt.

The village had already been patrolled by some Guardsmen, who found it empty. Now the tankers, together with a platoon of infantry from the Grenadier Guards, were to take possession of the southern end of the hamlet in what appeared to be a routine military chore.

They arrived before dawn and found the place empty. Being

British soldiers, they dismounted and began brewing up. It was then they heard the rumble of tanks from the direction of Zeven.

'I wonder if it's the Grenadiers?' Quinan asked. Unalarmed, he rose to his feet and focused his binoculars. At that instant an armour-piercing shell passed so close to his head that it blew off his beret. It was the Grenadiers all right, but not the British ones. These were the grenadiers of the German 15th Panzergrenadier Division under the command of *Leutnant* von Bülow; and Jurgen von Buelow, who would win the Iron Cross this day at Wistedt, had orders to throw the Tommies out of the place.

Now all hell broke loose. The Germans, who easily outnumbered the small British patrol, came in from all sides. Supported by mortar fire and their assault gun, they attacked through the line of trees that bordered the fields to the right of the road. (Even today one can dig the shrapnel out of the beams of the half-timbered farmhouses.) Things started to go badly wrong for the Micks. Their Firefly tank (a more powerful version of the Sherman and the only one of the four Allied tanks capable of tackling German armour) stalled. Its electrical system had failed. Quinan ordered the crew to bail out and told Charlton to dismantle the turret machine gun. They could use it to keep the Jerries at bay until help arrived. Then he radioed Major O'Cock for permission to withdraw. They were virtually surrounded and there was only one way of escape left to them – across the fields and through the woods. The Squadron Leader gave his approval – just in time. The Germans were within grenade-throwing distance. Quinan collected the able-bodied from the houses in which they had taken refuge and they set off, leaving the dead and dying behind them, with the panzergrenadiers already overruning their tanks in search of loot.

By this time Charlton was alone. Dick Sawtell, who had fled for cover with him, had been hit and wounded. Should he surrender? But the years with the Micks had paid off. Surrender was out of the question. He'd stick it out and fight on.

Delighted by the ease with which his grenadiers had overrun the Tommies, von Buelow pressed home his final attack only to find 'one enemy machine gun belabouring us with endless fire.' It was Eddie Charlton. For ten long minutes he held up the

Grenadiers' attack until a shell exploded nearby. He felt a searing pain in his left arm. Then it flopped to his side, totally useless. He had been badly hit. He struggled to a nearby fence where he propped up the Besa as best he could and opened fire once more. He was nearly knocked off his feet when he was hit again, but he reloaded and kept firing. He was hit for a third time and fell to the ground. There he was found by the Germans, and there he died.

That Saturday the lad from Lancashire won his country's most coveted award for bravery. It was to be the last Victoria Cross of the war in Europe.*

---

* Guardsman Charlton's body still rests in German soil some fifty miles from where he won his medal.

III

YOUNG MAN, I KILL THOUSANDS OF PEOPLE EVERY NIGHT

Guardsman Charlton's bravery would not be known till after the war when his comrades, who had been captured and released from German PoW camps testified to his outstanding courage. In the meantime, however, the appearance of the 15th Panzergrenadier in the gap between his XXX Corps and Ritchie's XII Corps worried Horrocks considerably. The last time his Intelligence people had heard of the Fifteenth it had been on his other flank facing the Highway Decorators. What were they up to now?

The situation worsened when fresh prisoners were brought in coming from the *Grossdeutschland* Division training brigade, another top-class German formation. So now Horrocks sweated it out awaiting the results of the RAF's attack on Bremen, due to start late that Saturday afternoon. Would the Germans surrender, or did this appearance of two German armoured formations on his right flank mean that General Becker was going to make a fight of it?

Herr Doktor Waldemar Seidel also sweated it out that day. He had eaten the last of his *Bratkartoffeln*, fried in castor oil, and finished his last two tins of sardines. Now he waited for the bombers which the surrender leaflets had said would come this day. His parents had been in Hanover when the Allies had threatened a similar raid if that city didn't surrender. It didn't and, as his parents had told him over the phone before it went dead, the result had been sixteen raids, one after another, which had wiped the former home of the English Hanoverian kings off the map. Now the Doctor, soon to be arrested by the Americans, prayed that the Tommies wouldn't use their feared block-busters, which were said to be able to penetrate ferro-concrete four metres thick. If they did, he wouldn't stand a chance.

He wasn't the only one waiting. Becker and the Nazi *Prominenz* were also counting the minutes as the long afternoon dragged by. Outside on the roofs of the bunkers and on their observation towers, the lookout, mostly 16-year-old boys from the Hitler Youth, searched the heavens with their glasses for the first signs of the enemy. Darkness started to fall. The search-lights clicked and parted the evening clouds with icy-white fingers. Still nothing. Were the Tommies coming or not?

Air Marshal Harris had commanded the RAF's Bomber Command since 1942. He never went on raids himself and often seemed to care as little about his crews as he did for the Germans they bombed. He was a 'hard case', who had learned his craft in the school of hard knocks in the Empire, where the fate of the 'wogs' he had helped to bomb into submission didn't matter one bit. Once, in 1944, he had been stopped for speeding in his large American car by a young policeman who obviously didn't recog-nize him. 'You could kill someone if you go on driving like that,' he said. To which the Air Marshal replied, 'Young man, I kill thousands of people every night!'

Harris thought he could win the war by bombing. Infantry were a thing of the past. In the end 56,000 of his men were killed in the attempt to prove him right, the heaviest loss of any service during the Second World War. To this day military historians are still arguing whether he was right or wrong.

Now he launched the first of his terrible raids on Bremen. That evening the sirens started to shrill and the citizens ran for their shelters as the first 'Christmas Trees', as they called the bunched flares, began to drift down. Out in the suburb of Vegesack one civilian watching them coming in, bomb doors already open, said, 'They were so low that you could count their four engines and nothing seemed to be stopping them.' It was true. Most of Bremen's 8th Falk Division was now engaged in a ground rôle ready to repel Horrocks' coming assault.

The RAF bomb aimers were notoriously bad when they had no 'pathfinders' to guide them and the first bombs fell wide. But not for long. The aimers soon got more accurate. After all, they were using the top-secret air-to-ground radar-aided sights. Their bombs fell on Bremen's industrial district, hitting shipping and motor-car plants. The dam on the Weser was also hit. Bremen had been planning to use the water held by the dam to flood the pastureland to the front of the city to make it impossible for the Tommies to use their armour. But it wasn't to be. Struck by twelve blockbusters, the pent-up water started to seep away harmlessly.

The terrified civilians in their air-raid shelters were no longer interested in General Becker and his plans for the defence of the city. Their sole aim was to survive. In the bunkers, now without power for lighting or smoke-and-air control, the temperatures started to rise alarmingly, some registering temperatures well over a hundred.

Now the RAF were coming in every twelve minutes to drop their deadly loads, and they came with impunity. There were no guns to stop them. Casualties began to mount alarmingly. Dr Waldemar Seidel, recorded his impressions that terrible night: 'The régime obviously wanted to be hated by their last supporters. How could women and children defend a city when their soldiers cowered underground for safety just as they did? Filthy, blackened by candle-flames, they looked at "their" soldiers and asked, "What was this heroic last defence all about?"'

The next day the RAF came again. Harris was determined to prove his long-held theory before he ran out of targets, for by now Allied fighter-bombers were also ranging far behind German lines with impunity, shooting up individual civilians, and they too were running out of better targets.

No one in authority listened to the complaints of the ordinary men and women in Bremen. Even if they had, there was nothing they could do about it. All of them feared for their own lives at the hands of the Gestapo and the frightening concept of *Sippenhaft** which applied to both high and low. That all that

* Automatic arrest and punishment of relatives of those the administration thought had betrayed their country.

was left to them was to pray for a speedy end to their misery and terror.

An air observer reported to Horrocks: 'In the centre of the town only the green leaden roofs of the Cathedral and the *Rathaus* stand and in one part there is *nothing* to be seen above ground at all for a mile in any direction.'

So the tower remained standing like an accusing finger pointed at heaven. It was an ironical reminder for those of the besiegers who knew that their forefathers had come from this very area and that an Englishman, St Willibald, had founded the church twelve centuries before and become Bremen's patron saint.

Unknown to Horrocks, on the second day of Harris's assault from the air a lowly infantry officer was trying to make the city surrender to him. That morning units of the 52nd Division, getting into the start position for the all-out assault on Bremen, captured the village of Achim after spending the night under German gunfire. Here, as he advanced to the still-standing red brick station, an enterprising young officer found that the special railway telephone to Bremen's main station was still working.

We do not know what went through his head as Harris's bombers rained death on Bremen's citizens once again. Chester Wilmot, the Australian war correspondent, was whistled up to observe for the BBC what might be an historic occasion. For the young subaltern and his Intelligence Officer had decided to do something which neither Horrocks, with his 100,000-man corps, nor Harris, with his thousands of bombers, had been able to do – get Bremen to surrender.

With Wilmot looking slightly out of place in military uniform, they convinced the station master to contact someone at Bremen's *Hauptbahnhof*. After some time a German lieutenant took up the phone at the other end and listened to what Wilmot called 'the British ultimatum' before going off to present it to General Becker. After an hour the lieutenant returned and said that no senior German officer would come to the phone to discuss terms and then added 'a friendly warning' that the RAF was bombing Bremen yet again. Then the phone went dead and there was nothing for them to do but trail back to their waiting jeeps. Before them, shrouded in smoke, was Bremen, a virtual island in the floodplain of the River Weser, protected to the south by a belt two miles wide and to the north-east and north by an area of low-lying ground laced with dykes and canals. A tough nut to crack. But that was the Corps Commander's problem.

4

28 APRIL – 5 MAY

I

JAPAN NEXT, I SUPPOSE, SIR

Now things started to move fast. DRs raced back and forth. Staff officers in jeeps hurried from HQ to HQ, on the lookout all the time for lone Hitler Youth kids out for some last glory. Armed with the lethal panzerfaust, they loved to pick off lone vehicles and their drivers before running home to mother, their part in the war already history. The tanks rumbled to their start lines and the infantry clambered aboard. Behind their guns, some of the gunners stripped to the waist, khaki handkerchiefs knotted about their cropped heads. The sappers came back to their lines, hands trembling slightly. All night they had been clearing mines and stringing out the white tapes indicating the mine-free areas through which the attackers would advance. And always in the fields to the rear the ambulance drivers lounged against their boxlike vehicles, pretending they didn't notice the cannon fodder filing by them in their hundreds.

Back at Horrocks' XXX Corps Headquarters, the phones rang all the time as red-tabbed staff officers pored over maps already covered with a rash of red and blue marks. Others dashed back and forth, issuing orders, ignoring the incessant jingle of the phones and the clatter of the teleprinter machines.

As usual, 'Jorrocks' wasn't there. He was up front with the waiting troops, as anxious as they were, but showing nothing of it as he gave the passing infantry, a smile and a wave of encouragement. He knew he would capture Bremen in the end, but how many of these boys would have to die in the process?

His plans had been laid ever since Montgomery's visit. The three-division attack would be kicked off by the Iron Division, which had by now closed up to the inundations bordering the

179

city. The Third had under command the 31st Armoured Brigade, consisting of the 4th/7th Dragon Guards, the 2nd Dragoons, the Buffaloes of the 4th Royal Tanks and Crocodiles of the 7th Royal Tanks. It was a formidable force. But Horrocks felt the Third needed additional muscle. After all, it would be advancing across waterlogged ground, which would keep the armour confined to the raised country roads, against a brigade of the 8th Flak Division equipped with deadly 88mm cannon. The Third would need every bit of extra help they could get.

The Royal Norfolks, the Ulster Rifles and the Shropshire Light Infantry set off in their Buffaloes in the moonlight. The opposite back of the Weser was quiet. The assault infantry could hardly believe that more than 3,000 German infantry were waiting for them on the far side of the river. But they knew in their hearts that they wouldn't get away with it much longer.

They were right. Halfway across and still praying they were going to make it, the assault infantry were alerted by the first flare. It was the signal. Tracer zipped across the surface of the water. A machine gun chattered. Somewhere a mortar gave a grunt and the first bomb rose into the air to come down in the Weser. Battle had been joined!

With the Buffalo drivers zigzagging as best they could, the first of the troop carriers slammed into the muddy bank. The infantry did not need an order. They scrambled out and up, firing from the hip as they went. Then they blundered across the water-logged fields heading for the German strongpoints.

Two light flak guns guarding a bridge held them up. They spat a white wall of fire, pouring hundreds of shells at the advancing Tommies. But the men didn't go to ground. There was no cover of any value anyway. They charged at the guns and the gunners fled or died at their weapons.

But it wasn't going to be a walkover, the men soon realized that. Even after most of the guns of the 8th Flak Division had been knocked out there were still small parties of fanatics every-where in the ruins all too ready to die.

Just after the men of the Ulster Rifles had dealt with the German cannon the leading platoon of the KOSB, commanded by young Peter Lloyd, came under fire. They had been clearing a small enemy barracks near the village of Habenhausen when,

180

as Lloyd recalled after the war, 'Suddenly we were sniped from the right flank. We were completely exposed on this flank. I could hear the bullets whining very close and hugged the ground frantically. The terrifying thing was we couldn't locate this solitary sniper. A man lying close to me was hit in the head and died shortly afterwards. Each of us tried to crawl as best we could to safety. Then another man was hit in the arm. Try as I could, I could not locate the fire and the platoon behind us could not pin it down directly.'

By now the harassed young officer and his surviving men dare not raise their heads an inch above the ground. The unknown sniper seemed to dominate the whole area. The slightest movement was noted and followed a second later by a head-shattering bullet.

'Our Piat man had been hit too. I wriggled as best I could to a small wall in order to get protection from the enemy, who was picking us off one by one. I could hear the ping of bullets all the time and the shots seemed very close indeed. However, I managed to reach the wall all right. Then a cry from H, "They've hit me." He went lunging past, clasping his arm and making a run for it.' Lloyd seized the opportunity. 'I got to my feet and ran, ran as hard as I could.'

So Lloyd survived to tell his tale. But that day there were children who would never live to tell their tale, or, if they did survive, would be traumatized by it for the rest of their lives. As one 8-year-old girl remembered fifty years later, 'A terrible artillery bombardment set in. It was so bad that we couldn't run to the shelter. Half an hour later the first British tanks started to roll through the streets. We ran upstairs. All our windows were broken. My uncle sat up in bed, covered in bits of glass, but unhurt.' As the little girl looked outside, she saw 'dead every-where. That was the worst half-hour of the war for me'.

Horst Biese had come to Bremen two years earlier to start his apprenticeship at the Flying School near the suburb of Sebaldsbruck. He was 14. Like most of his fellow apprentices, he was a fanatical member of the Hitler Youth and worshipped the Führer. Now, as the Tommies launched their all-out attack, he was ordered to drop his file and wire brush and pick up a panzerfaust. Like the rest of the apprentices, he had exactly twenty-four hours to learn how to use it. Like the rest, he did so with alacrity. Now they were going to be allowed to fight for the Führer.

That Sunday, 22 April, 'We went to pick up a panzerfaust, a rifle and a bicycle. Then we rode off to find the battlefield.' But they couldn't find it. All afternoon Horst lay in somebody's garden and waited for the English to come so that he could earn an Iron Cross. But there was no medal for him, that day.

In the end the battle found Biese and his twenty comrades as they attempted to defend the Railway Repair Yard at Sebaldsbruck. Shells were falling all around them and by the time the artillery softening-up had ended five of Biese's fellow apprentices were dead and the courage of the rest was broken. The survivors made a run for it, but didn't get far. Machine-gun fire scythed their ranks. Biese went down next to a wounded Tommy who was writhing with pain, a great hole in his right arm where he had been shot.

Moments later Biese himself was shot in the arm. Somehow he struggled to his feet and fled down the body-littered street to a house where they knew what to do. The civilians tugged off his uniform, cut it into small pieces and carefully fed the pieces into the toilet, where, fortunately, the flush was still working. Thereafter he was sent to hospital to have his arm treated, and there he remained for another three months until he was released into a totally different world.

Today, as a 68-year-old pensioner, he remembers those days with bitter feelings, realizing yet again how his generation had been sold by the Party under Hitler, fooled by a creed that meant nothing. Later 'as I realized what had happened, I cried and cried, and cried again. We who lived in the belief that we were an élite knew that we had been betrayed.' Today all that remains of that time is a damaged arm which, for over half a century, he has never been able to use properly.

The men of the King's Shropshire Light Infantry took their objective at bayonet point, one of the last bayonet charges of the war. One company was led by a man who should really have been back at Battalion Headquarters. He was Private Wood, of Intelligence, who went ahead of the infantry through the smoke and fog of war, shouting at the dug-in German infantry waiting for the assault to come out and surrender.

The Germans launched a last counter-attack against the Norfolks, who had dug in around a newly captured German barracks. Prisoners had told them that the defenders, the surviving SS of the 18th Horst Wessel Training and Replacement Battalion, had fled. They might well have done so, but other Germans had infiltrated the barracks and now they counter-attacked. But the Norfolks were ready for them, so they didn't get far. Soon the steam went out of their attack which now settled down to the usual costly slogging match.

On the Iron Division's front the heart had also gone out of the German defenders and to the south of the floods the 2nd Lincolns had fought their last battle of the war without their CO, up front with his men, finding a suitable target at which to shoot.

They captured their final objective, the airfield, which had been defended by the survivors of the Marine Infantry Division, now down to a mere 3,000 men and beginning their retreat northwards. Those they had left behind alive were now the Norfolks' captives.

Standing in the late afternoon sunshine, Major Glyn Gilbert, commander of the Norfolks' 'C' Company, was in a reflective mood. The campaign had been too long and too hard. Too many good men had died. With an ex-U-boat commander, who had led the Marines, he watched as they began their march to the cage.

'Under a Petty Officer they then marched past us, carrying their wounded. The Commander called out the equivalent of "Well done" and received a spontaneous and tremendous cheer from his seamen. We then saluted each other and he followed them into captivity.'

Later the Major recalled, 'I have never forgotten the incident. This German officer and his men provided a perfect example of leadership and high morale at a time when their country was in ruins and their future unknown.'

But the introspective moment soon passed as his old friend CSM Sam Smalley appeared and remarked, 'That's about it then.' Gilbert agreed. They had fired their last round in Europe.

Soon they'd be engaging a totally different kind of enemy, in Palestine, the sacrificial goats of both sides of that particular conflict.

Gilbert reflected that, 'There were five of us left in 'C' Company who had landed in Normandy in June last year and I remember feeling suddenly very tired and sad about the casualties we had suffered in the last few hours. I did not realize it at the time, but I was the only rifle company commander in the Division who had landed on D-Day and had not been killed or wounded.

But the Sergeant-Major soon drove such thoughts from his head. 'Japan next, I suppose,' he said.

II

WE BRITISH ALWAYS WIN

Horrocks had watched that last attack of the 3rd Division on Bremen's airfield. He joined two young gunner-observation officers in the attic of a bomb-shattered house, overlooking the flooded fields. To be a gunner forward observer was one of the most dangerous jobs in the Army. Once the shells they had directed on the enemy landed, the latter were usually able to work out from where the FOs were observing and bring down the whole weight of their fire on the observation post.

But that worried neither the Corps Commander nor the two young officers. The latter were too busy bringing down fire on German anti-tank guns which were holding up XXX Corps tanks to notice who was crouching next to them in the attic. As Horrocks wrote after the war, 'For a few minutes I was able to forget the problems of a corps battle and lose myself in this front-line duel which was unfolding before my eyes.'

Suddenly it was all over. The German guns were pointing into the air and the young gunners were dancing round the loft crying, 'Got them! Direct hit!' Horrocks took a last look. They were right. The tanks of the 4th/7th Dragoon Guards were moving forward once more. The General stole away, leaving the gunners to their triumph, knowing he had to return to the grim reality of directing nearly 100,000 men in battle.

Now he had to commit the bulk of his corps to battle. On his left flank he had the protection of the Weser, now firmly held by the 3rd Division. Further to the west, on the same flank, the 2nd Canadian, the Polish Armoured Division and the 51st Highland were keeping *Korps Ems* too busy to have any real influence on the battle for Bremen. So now Horrocks could commit the 52nd

Lowland Division and then the 43rd Wessex on the right flank. There was only one catch. If in the gap between his and Ritchie's XII Corps, patrolled at the moment only by the Guards Armoured and the 52nd Reconnaissance Regiment, the Germans broke loose in any strength, then his two infantry divisions would be in trouble. But that was a risk he had to take. Again the Top Brass were breathing down his neck. Time was running out and he couldn't afford to hesitate. He gave the 52nd and then the 43rd the order to start their advance into the heart of the city.

The 52nd Lowland Division's assault started quietly enough. At four o'clock on the morning of 23 April two companies of the Sixth Battalion, the King's Own Scottish Borderers started to advance up the narrow country road between the villages of Bierden and Uphusen. They were to be the van of the 20,000-strong division – a handful of older officers and teenage soldiers reaching out on their own until they hit the enemy. Then it would all start.

Neither of the two company commanders had seen the ground by daylight and all that Major Stewart, commander of the KOSB's 'A' Company, had to guide him was an aerial photograph. Naturally it was pretty useless in the glowing darkness. His task was to negotiate a scrubby rise and take his first objective – an old flak site once used for the anti-aircraft defence of Bremen. So he and his young soldiers moved in alternative sections on either side of the road. Since the aerial photo had been taken the enemy had built a fairly strong defensive position in the area, complete with wire and machine-gun nests. In addition, the flak site had been reoccupied by the Germans. The KOSBs were walking into a trap.

Now it started to rain, but the Scots were used to that. They pressed on up the road, no sound save that of their harsh breathing and inevitable clink of the tin mugs strapped to their small pack. To their flank 'C' Company advanced on the same objective. Steadily the Scots advanced to meet the challenge which would surely come.

Unknown to the KOSBs, things were already going wrong for them. The area of the initial attack was packed with gun batteries, headquarters, command posts and the like, all linked by radios more powerful than the 18 sets used by the infantry. Now with those radios chattering incessantly, as messages were sent back and forth, the KOSB's Battalion HQ soon lost contact with their leading two companies.

At Battalion HQ this had been expected. The 18 set, like the three-ton truck, also defective and underpowered, was one of the criminally negligent products of British industry during the Second World War. Still the battalion commander, knowing all this, was worried. In the little farmhouse HQ the staff chain-smoked and waited for news. Time and again the officers rounded on the tense signallers as they tried to raise the missing companies.

Just after first light the officers were startled by the scream of a German MG 42. Almost immediately the fire was returned by short bursts from British Brens. The officers looked at each other. The two missing companies had bumped into the opposition.

'C' Company had been first to run into trouble. They had bumped almost head-on into the German 280th Infantry Battalion, which outnumbered them four to one. The 280th was a so-called 'Stomach Battalion', because it contained a large number of combat-experienced soldiers who were grouped together due to illness, so their special dietary needs could be catered for.

But if their stomachs were not altogether right, they possessed a great deal of what the British Army called 'intestinal fortitude', otherwise known as 'guts'. They lammed into 'C' Company and soon the radio links were full of calls for help: 'Jerry still in occupation.' 'Taking heavy Spandau fire.' 'Intercepted message from 'C' Company, state they're cut off from the rear.' 'C' Company was in what the Battalion CO, Colonel Davidson, called later 'a sticky situation'.

They were. The Stomach Battalion was within ten yards of the wooden huts in which the 'C' Company men had taken cover. They tried to blast the trapped Jocks from their positions with panzerfausts. The rockets were followed by bursts of machine-gun fire at the closest range as the Germans tried to rip the flimsy huts apart.

In the hut which housed 'C' Company's HQ bullets ricochetted round the room. Plaster fell from the ceiling like snow. Chunks of wood and brick spurted from the shattered walls as the Germans hosed the place with fire. Frantically the signallers dug up the floorboards with their jackknives in an attempt to bury their precious radios, their only link with the outside world.

Not realizing that HQ knew their position from 'A' Company's signal, Lieutenant Harry Atkinson, who had won the Military Medal for bravery as an NCO, volunteered to bring help. He slipped out of the back door into the dawn and vaulted a fence into the yard. Then the German machine gunners spotted him. The tracer swept towards him and he dropped to the cobbles, as if hit. For fifteen minutes he lay there shamming dead as the tracer whipped over his head.

Finally, judging it time to move, he slipped off his pack and taking a deep breath, he was up and running. By eight o'clock he had convinced his CO that the forward companies needed more muscle. At the double Colonel Davidson brought up his other two companies. But Davidson still wasn't convinced he had sufficient strength. So he asked for a divisional 'shoot' and armoured support.

The divisional artillery commander responded at once. Every gun available, from 8-inch howitzer to 3-inch mortar, slammed into action. The noise was ear-splitting. The very ground trembled and fountains of earth erupted. Then, as suddenly as it had started, the barrage ceased. At once the KOSBs were moving forward again, this time supported by tanks from the Royal Scots Greys and a troop of mobile flame-throwing Crocodile tanks.

The outskirts of Uphusen were soon secured by the infantry. The Crocodiles waddled in, towing their fuel containers behind them. The Greys took up their positions to cover the fire-spitting monsters. The gunners had seen the dreadful results of their labours before, but it had to be done. The flames shot from the muzzles and curled around the houses held by the Germans. At this range the impact of the flames was horrific. In that terrible half hour the men of the Stomach Battalion took murderous casualties. But the Jocks pressed home their attack. As one eyewitness recorded, 'The attack was one hundred percent successful. The Jocks tore through the town, pitching the Huns out of their holes, while the Crocodiles roasted and the tanks blasted them out of the buildings. D Company followed, yelling and cheering for all they were worth.'

By midday that Monday the Stomach Battalion had ceased to exist. All that was left of them, some 150 frightened prisoners, were hustled to the rear and the advance on Bremen continued.

The Division's 52nd Reconnaissance Regiment had been warned by their CO, Colonel Hankey, to expect an exciting time ahead as they had set off on their long swing round the right flank of Horrocks' XXX Corps from Verden. The CO had been right. Even as the regiment formed up in Verden's main street heading for Bremen, German jet fighter-bombers had fallen out of the sky and attempted to beat up the tightly packed column of vehicles. Fortunately the pilots were inexperienced and zigzagged back and forth across the vehicles instead of coming in from the front and shooting up the whole column.

Since then it had been one minor skirmish and holding action after another, with the regiment spread out in small groups, more often than not commanded by NCOs who had to make their decisions on the spot. It had been a slow progress – indeed it would take them seven days to cover the 20 miles to the outskirts of the city. They had been bombarded by massed 88mms. They had been attacked by panzerfaust-wielding Hitler Youths. Once they had caught two kids, led by an older man, trying to cut their signal wire to the rear. The troopers were all for shooting all three there and then. But the sergeant in charge had simply cuffed the defiant youths and yelled, 'Now go home to yer frigging mother'.

Then one small patrol of members of the anti-tank troop, still towing their six-pounder cannon, which was absolutely useless against German armour, heard the rumble of tank tracks to their front. Two of the troop volunteered to try and find out whether the tanks were British or German. Armed solely with sten guns, they tracked the mysterious tanks till dawn when they veered off into some woods and vanished. It was then that they discovered the tanks were indeed German – but there *were* no enemy tanks in this section of the 52nd's front!

This, and the fact that the Guards Armoured Division, engaged in operations north of Zeven and around the Allied POW camp at Wesertimke, which the Guards had just liberated, were meeting ever greater opposition from the 15th Panzer-grenadier Division, must have given Horrocks' staff officers pause for thought. Were the Germans going to launch a large-scale counter-attack? As we have already seen, not only the 15th Panzergrenadier but also the *Grossdeutschland* had been iden-tified in that area. An attack of that nature would jeopardize the whole Bremen operation. *

The Guards, who were bearing the brunt of the firing on that flank, were seemingly not worried. That evening the mixed force of Scots and Welsh Guards who had liberated the 8,000 mainly British seamen PoWs at Wesertimke had their hands full trying to keep some semblance of order inside the camp. Already men cooped up for many years had cut through the wire and disappeared on their own private missions, in which finding a woman loomed large. Everywhere inside the camp there were chicken feathers, indicating that for some love went through the stomach. In the next few days there would be a noticeable decrease in the hen population in the villages around the camp.

Forty Guardsmen, who had been PoWs inside the camp, were now given their captors' rifles and told to keep order, but it was hopeless. In the end the Guards gave up, let their fellow PoWs loot and enjoyed the spectacle, especially that of a 'very dark' West Indian Merchant Navy fireman. He was wearing a looted bowler, smoked a large cigar and was very drunk. As he rode around on his 'liberated' bike he proudly announced, 'We British always win'.

* In fact the 15th Panzergrenadier was holding up the Guards in order that other non-motorized units of the *Korps Ems* could escape north before XXX and XII Corps joined up.

III

I HAD THE GREATEST DIFFICULTY
IN RESTRAINING HIM

At two o'clock on the morning of 26 April, while the weary men of the Iron Division slept, now that their part in the battle was over, an officer appeared at the battered police station at No.3 Hemelinger Strasse and demanded of the surprised elderly *Schupos* that they put him in touch with someone senior. But the lines were down everywhere. The three days of fighting had taken their toll. Finally the policeman managed to raise Bremen's Main Police HQ on an emergency line. There it was hastily agreed with the unknown British officer that a German police officer would bring General Fritz Becker to the phone in one hour's time.

So they waited while, outside in the glowing darkness, the guns still boomed. The British were now using their field artillery in the city centre, firing over open sights. All were weary and dirty. There had been no running water for forty-eight hours, but still they were alert, one ear cocked to where the phone stood. At three o'clock precisely, as agreed, it started to ring. The police sergeant in charge grabbed it and held it to his ear. He listened intently. Then his face fell. Instinctively the British officer knew what had happened – Becker had refused to surrender, even though the city hadn't a chance. He was right. Becker had flatly resisted coming to the phone to discuss surrender terms. He knew his situation was hopeless, but he had just received an order to withdraw all troops not currently engaged and send them to join Field Marshal Busch's troops further north to help man the next line of defence. For their sake he thought he should fight on.

The officer gave in. Becker had had his last chance. He shook hands with the equally dismayed cops and went slowly out into the night. Faintly now he could hear pipes and wondered what was going on. Who was playing pipes in the middle of this mayhem? It was Piper Jock Gray leading the KOSBs into the shattered streets of Bremen's onetime business district. Suddenly the night was full of the sound of 'Hawick's Queen of the Borders' and 'Joddart's Here'. The KOSBs were going into their last battle.

Not far away Brigadier 'Joe' Vandeleur, who had led that abortive push to link up with the trapped 1st Airborne in Arnhem seven months before, was wide awake. He was putting the final touches to his plan of attack. His 129th Brigade of the 43rd Division had been given the 'honour' of capturing the *Burgerpark*, a stronghold in the northern part of the city.

Vandeleur's orders from 'Butcher' Thomas, the ruthless commander of the 43rd, were to clear out Bremen east of the railway line which bisected it and then advance on the *Burgerpark*. Already the place, where eight roads met, was known to the troops as 'Piccadilly Circus', but what the rank and file didn't yet know was that the park housed a series of powerful bunkers hidden from the air by trees. The main bunker was the headquarters of Major-General Sibert, second-in-command to Becker, also the headquarters of the Flak Artillery. Knock out that bunker, the 43rd's staff officers reasoned, and Becker would be without firepower.

But Vandeleur was not too happy with the assignment. It could be costly, especially as he was reluctant to use the Crocodile tanks. But Thomas was adamant. So he decided to keep Colonel Lipscomb's Somerset Light Infantry in reserve and then, once the park had been reached, to launch them after darkness 'to smash our way into the big bunkers where the German HQ and core of their defences were situated'.

In bright daylight the 1,200 men of the 4th and 5th Wiltshires started to advance in an extended line towards their objective. Advancing by a complicated system of companies leap-frogging companies, they took their first, second, third and fourth objectives without too much trouble. The Brigadier was happy. Everything was going to plan.

At seven-thirty that morning the two lead companies clattered towards their sixth objective in their Bren-gun carriers. Then the advance was brought to a halt by a hastily erected structure of domestic furniture and wooden beams. It caused them little trouble, but as the infantry dismounted to tackle the obstacle two youths armed with Spandaus emerged. 'These two heroes,' as one of the Wiltshires said, 'were given a swift kick up the arse and sent packing. We couldn't be bothered to take prisoners.'

The advance continued. A seven-storey flak tower barred their progress. It was surrounded by high blast walls and looked a tough nut to crack. They need not have worried. The defenders surrendered without a shot being fired. It was going to be a walkover.

Suddenly a German quadruple flak cannon opened up from a side street. A stream of 20mm tracer shells raced towards the Wiltshires who went to ground as one, lying flat on the cobbles as the shells hissed above their heads. They radioed for help and didn't have to wait long. A forty-ton Churchill tank rumbled up, armed with a strange sawn-off cannon. The infantry recognized it as one of 'Churchill's funnies'.

It fired one of its huge bunker-breaking mortar bombs and the flak cannon disappeared in a flash of yellow light, the crew flying in all directions.

Road block after road block was taken. Here and there some lone hero tried to stop the triumphant advance, but to no avail. Nothing seemed able to stop the Wiltshires. It was mid-afternoon when they reached the outskirts of the park, the prewar pride and joy of the city's prosperous citizens.

Now the Wiltshires ran into some German marines, whom Brigadier Vandeleur later called 'lusty fighters'. They started taking casualties. Major Colverson of 'A' Company ran straight into German machine-gun fire and was killed on the spot. The CO, Colonel Corbyn, hurried up to assess the situation.

Angry at being stalled, he called down artillery fire, which, in that built-up area, was difficult to direct accurately. A shell fell short and Colonel Corbyn went down. He was the third colonel of the Wiltshires to be killed or wounded in the campaign.

Vandeleur didn't like using the Crocodiles. They went against his principles, especially as there were still plenty of civilians in the area. But in the end, with Thomas breathing down his neck, he called them up.

The 5th Wiltshires were still advancing, but they were also running into trouble, stopped by firing from the same barracks which was holding up the 4th. Up front a Lieutenant Blackman was undeterred by the small-arms fire streaming their way. He rolled forward in his carrier, ready for anything. He was in luck. They came across a badly frightened German *landser*, whose hands shot into the air at the first sight of the men in khaki. '*Kamerad*,' he cried. A moment later ninety-seven of his *Kameraden* appeared and surrendered to the young officer without further ado.

But the next time Blackman's section stopped it was by a different type of enemy who weren't prepared to surrender so easily. A fire fight broke out and Blackman, mindful that the end of the war was near and that he didn't want to lose any more men at this stage, whistled up the Shermans of the supporting Sherwood Foresters who went smartly into action. They plastered the enemy with 75mm cannon, and soon the German survivors had had enough of the uneven battle.

By now the Crocodiles had arrived on the scene. As Brigadier Vandeleur and the CO of the Somerset Light Infantry waited, they advanced and set to work on the houses holding up the advance. Captain Hancock, a gunner observing for the SLI, wrote afterwards, 'It was a grand sight to watch the Crocodiles belching great tongues of flame 70 or 80 yards long and in a short time both houses were burning furiously. The Boche inside had an unpleasant choice; the flames within or the waiting machine guns of our infantry and tanks outside. The roads were littered with branches of trees and smashed buses and civilian cars, destroyed in the preliminary bombardment. The battle was now well under control with the tanks, Crocodiles and infantry providing mutual covering fire as together they assaulted house after house.'

Brigadier Vandeleur was carried away by the sight. As Colonel Lipscomb of the Somersets recorded, 'The Brigadier, who is an Irishman, found the thirst for battle almost too much for him. I had great difficulty in restraining him from joining the attacking company's leading section.'

Others too were mesmerized by this spectacle. One eye witness recorded, 'The battle which ensued was almost appalling in its magnificence. Burning houses cast a lurid light over the flame-throwers as they slowly waddled up the streets and by the infantry as they dashed from house to house.'

Soon 'Hyde Park Corner', as this section was called, was taken. The Somersets, exhausted by the battle for the cross-roads, slumped down on the battle-littered pavements and took a rest. It was now that Major Beckhurst of the Somersets bumped into Major Pope of the 4th Wiltshires. The cheerful young Wiltshire Major, who affected a huge RAF-style moustache, was reconnoitring the area. Now he pointed out a large concrete bunker which rose over thirty feet above the park. It seemed to both officers worth investigating. So they set off together in search of they knew not what.

Others were wandering around too, like soldiers do who have survived a battle and are curious to know where they are and what was going on before they put a sudden end to the lives of the people who had lived there. Private Bob Thornburrow of the Somerset Light Infantry moved into a Party bunker and was welcomed by the bizarre sight of a high-ranking Nazi official and his wife who had both committed suicide. There was a Luger pistol and an empty brandy bottle between them on the blood-soaked carpet. Naturally he took the Luger. In a prosperous shipbuilder's house Brigadier Vandeleur found a copy of Hitler's *Mein Kampf*. As Captain John Merdith recorded, 'The Brigadier wrote on the fly-leaf, "This illuminating volume is left to you by courtesy of the British Liberation Army. If you can believe it, you can believe anything. It is left in hope that you will study its follies in the years to come."'

Meanwhile the two infantry officers had reached the mysterious bunker. It was adorned with a huge eagle and swastika. In front of it were arranged two lines of British bombs of all sizes which had been dropped on Bremen over the last four years and had failed to explode.

As the last group of 2,771 prisoners which the Wiltshires had taken during the last thirty-six hours streamed gratefully into the divisional cages, Pope and Beckhurst went from room to room of the big bunker, their boots echoing on the uncarpeted floor. The place was a regular rabbit-warren. Smaller rooms and mysterious staircases ran off in every direction. All was confusion. There were discarded weapons and equipment on all sides.

Now joined by a handful of infantrymen, they pushed on. They came across fourteen German soldiers lying on the bare floor, all wounded and abandoned. They continued down a small corridor, illuminated by weak yellow lights enclosed in wire cages. They opened a door to find thirty or so German officers seated round a large wooden table, piled high with empty champagne bottles. The Jerries, it seemed, had been celebrating their defeat.

But where was Becker?

IV

SHUT UP, YOU SON OF A BITCH.
HE'S BEEN REHEARSING THIS
ALL HIS LIFE

On the same night that the two British officers looked for the missing Becker in that gloomy command bunker, 700 miles to the south the Top Brass of the US 7th Army were making plans for the capture of one last, if useless, prestige objective – Hitler's private lair in the Bavarian Alps, the Berghof.

Quite recently it had been reduced to a virtual ruin by the RAF. Still the Brass thought that its capture – even minus the Führer, who had only a handful of days to go before he committed suicide in Berlin – was worth it. By now, after the capture of Munich, with surrender negotiations in the south already in full swing, this was about the last prize left to them. The fact that its capture would cost yet more young American lives presumably didn't occur to them. Personal glory was paramount in these last days of the war in Europe.

The trouble was there were too many contenders for the prize, including Patton himself. Fortunately, by changing army boundaries, his Third Army was cut out of the race and the dash for the Berghof was left, at first anyway, to O'Daniel's Third Infantry Division of the US Seventh Army. But there were other contenders for the Berghof trophy. They were the 'Screaming Eagles', the 101st Airborne Division, and, as yet unknown to the American brass, the French.

The tankers of General Leclerc's 2nd French Armoured Division now set off to beat the other two Allied divisions to the

'Eagle's Nest, as the Americans insisted on calling the Berghof. The 7th Army Commander, Patch, found out about it and told Leclerc, 'You've had Paris and you've had Strasbourg. You can't expect Berchtesgaden as well.' But Leclerc felt he could.

But O'Daniel wasn't to be cheated of the honour and he ordered the bridges and roads to be guarded and reserved only for his 'Marnemen' of the Third Infantry Division. Leclerc's French dodged them, as did the 'Screaming Eagles', and the French then barred all the roads up to the mountain eyrie. The boot was now on the other foot. Then the American and French commanders agreed on a compromise. At a joint ceremony at the Berghof both the French and American flags would fly over the ruins for the benefit of the newsreel men.

So they went ahead with the ceremony. There was the raising of the flags, speeches, saluting, presenting of arms, bands playing the two national anthems, and then, at a critical point, the French flag suddenly fell down, leaving 'Old Glory' to wave alone over the Berghof. In years to come no one was ever able to explain just why the French flag had fallen down. If O'Daniel had a hand in it, he took that secret with him to the grave. But there it was, the American flag fluttering in triumph over the beaten 1,000 Year Reich, alone in its glory. The US Army had captured its last prestige objective, which had served no military or political purpose at all, save, if you wish, to provide a convenient holiday camp for US troops stationed in Germany for the next half a century.

The final capture of General Fritz Becker had a much more profound effect on the outcome of the war than the capture of the Berghof. The day before he surrendered he signalled Field Marshal Busch's HQ: 'Infantry attacks beaten off. No ammunition left. Fighting on with last remaining elements. Long live the Führer.' It was the spirit of Stalingrad, which the Führer had admired so greatly two years earlier. Even as Becker's staff officers were urging to him to surrender, he had threatened anyone who attempted to do so with 'a bullet in the back of the skull'.

Now, on the final day of the Battle of Bremen, accompanied by a staff officer and a British PoW, Becker went tamely out of his HQ to surrender to the British. Time and again he had declared he would fight to the end, whatever the cost, even that of his own life.* But he went tamely into the PoW cage, with his batman carrying his luggage. Clearly he had never really intended to die for his Führer.

As the battle came to an end and the British spread through the rest of Bremen, some fifty miles away in Hamburg, Major General Wolz sweated. He was Becker's equivalent, the Battle Commandant of the city. For two weeks he too had been expecting an all-out attack on the city. After all the British lined the whole length of the River Elbe which ran to Hamburg's front. But, like Becker, he had been undecided what to do.

The city itself was defended by a collection of military flotsam – Army, Marines, Luftwaffe, even Hungarians. The Party, which really controlled the city, blew hot and cold about defending Hamburg, and Wolz was terrified of the *Sippenhaft* if he surrendered. But Becker's submission in Bremen changed all that.

The local businessman, a real power in Hamburg, the Party *Prominenz* and the commanders of the defence force, which, in addition to the city itself, were also in charge of a long stretch of the Elbe to the east, then lost heart. They didn't want to see what was left of the great city destroyed like Bremen under Becker. They wanted peace.

The negotiations between Wolz and the British started at the lowest level: staff officers of the 7th Armoured Division and civilians and officers from the Hamburg garrison. They met in a *gasthaus* in a remote hamlet outside the city. At the end of the first talks one of the German civilians asked a 7th Armoured Brigadier, 'Will we be sent to Siberia? Should I and the rest of the staff commit suicide?' The Brigadier answered gravely, 'That's entirely up to you.'

On the same day that Leclerc and O'Daniel bickered about who should have the honour of taking the ruined shell on the top of the mountain overlooking Berchtesgaden the talks had been moved up a notch or two. Now they were between Field Marshal Busch and Monty's staff. Other talks, between the leading men in the intimate circle of the new 'Führer', Grand

---

* He died in his bed 22 years later and was given a military funeral by the new German *Bundeswehr* as an example to the 'young recruits of the *Bundeswehr*'.

Admiral Doenitz, and 2nd Army's senior Intelligence Officers, followed.

On the day the French flag fell down at the Berghof the surrender delegation arrived at Montgomery's tented HQ in the middle of nowhere. Suddenly Montgomery's rôle had been transformed from that of an insignificant flank guard to Bradley's US armies to one in which he would accept the surrender of all of Germany's surviving armies.

It was a moment of great triumph and one which he savoured to the full. He looked at the head of the German surrender team with his piercing blue eyes and said in a sharp voice, 'Who are you?'

Admiral von Friedeburg, who had once thought himself *so* important, almost broke down. But he pulled himself together and stuttered, '*Grossadmiral* von Friedeburg, sir. Commander-in-Chief of the Germany Navy, sir.'

Montgomery looked at him contemptuously. It had taken him five long years to reach this moment. Now at his cruellest, he snapped, 'Never heard of you.'

Listening to the exchange one of his 'eyes and ears'* whispered to his neighbour, Major Dawnay, that the 'old man' was putting up 'a good show'. Dawnay hissed back, 'Shut up, you son of a bitch. He's been rehearsing this all his life.'

Montgomery had. Now he was ready to make the Hun pay. He wanted the lot. Not just Hamburg, not even the whole of Northern Germany and Denmark. He wanted, and would get, the surrender of that whole Nazi empire. It was the little Field Marshal's finest hour.

---

* Montgomery's young Canadian, British and American liaison officers.

APPENDIX

According to Anglo-American author Cornelius Ryan, who first went into the details of the top-secret *Operation Eclipse* in some detail in his book *The Last Battle*, the first mention of the plan was made by German sources in January, 1945. According to Ryan, a Captain von Bila, an aide to General Heinrici, later the defender of Berlin, came across 'Eclipse' in the High Command's HQ in Zossen in East Germany. It had, Ryan learnt through von Bila, been captured from the British at a front CP in the last stage of the Battle of the Bulge in the fourth week of January, 1945.

A local German historian, Herbert Schwarzwalder of Bremen, maintains, to the contrary, that the 'Eclipse' plan was first reported to the German High Command by General Blumentritt and Colonel-General Blaskowitz a month or so later. Again the plan was captured from a British source, this time from a wrecked armoured car captured by German paras of General Student's 1st Parachute Army.

But in either case the question remains uppermost: what would a top-secret plan be doing in the front line? General 'Slim Jim' Gavin, the wartime commander of 82nd Airborne Division, thought the plan originated from another source altogether. He wrote that he believed the details of the plan came from the Russians, who fed it to the Germans, presumably to confuse them or make them fight harder in the west against those which would turn postwar Germany into a rural backwater; this, naturally, would be of advantage to the Red Army advancing from the east.

As Gavin saw it, a Russian spy in either Washington or

Eisenhower's HQ originally obtained the plan for the Russians. General Sir Kenneth Strong, Eisenhower's wartime chief-of-intelligence, asked to comment on this theory by the present author, answered, 'It seems to me that Gavin is looking at 1944/45 events in the climate of present-day Russo-American relations'. Strong felt that the 'innuendo' that there was a Russian spy in Washington or in Eisenhower's HQ had no foundation in fact.

Now these problems still remain: (1) What would a British fighting unit be doing with it at the front? (2) When was it obtained and how? (3) Why, when all such documents were numbered and registered as a matter of form, was 'Operation Eclipse', or a copy of it, never reported as missing?

Thus it remains a minor, perhaps even a major, mystery of the Second World War which has never been resolved, although the missing documents make a nonsense of all the books written on the Eisenhower capture of Berlin controversy of March, 1945.

BIBLIOGRAPHY

C. Barclay, *The History of the 53rd Welch Division in the Second World War* (London, 1956)

G. Blacker, *Mountain and Flood* (Glasgow, 1952)

M. Cunliffe, *History of the Royal Warwickshire Regiment* (London, 1956)

P. Delaforce, *Red Crown and Dragon* (Stroud, 1997)

K. Doenitz, *Zehn Jahre und Zwanzig Tage* (Bonn, 1954)

J. Dunlop, *The Capitulation of Hamburg* (Journal of the Royal United Services Institute)

L. Ellis, *The Welsh Guards at War* (Aldershot, 1946)

Edited, *Geschichte des Panzerkorps Grossdeutschland* (Neckargemund, 1956)

H. Gunning, *The War History of the King's Own Scottish Borderers* (Berwick on Tweed, 1948)

R. Peters, *Zwolf Jahre Bremen* (Bremen, 1951)

J. Russell, *No Triumphant Procession* (London)

J. Salmod, *The History of 51st Highland Division* (Edinburgh, 1951)

N. Scarfe, *Assault Division: A History of the 3rd Division* (London, 1957)

L. Steiner, *Die 23 Tage der Regierung Doenitz* (Düsseldorf, 1967)

BBC War Reports (London, 1945)

C. Whiting, *48 Hours to Hammelburg* (New York, 1971)

C. Whiting and W Trees, *Die Amis Sind Da* (Aachen, 1975)

Divisional Histories: 1st, 30th, 3rd, 63rd, 45th, 100th US Infantry Divisions; 3rd, 5th, 7th, 10th, 4th Armored Divisions.

INDEX

211

THE THIRD INFANTRY DIVISION